Signalman's Reflections

C000060145

Signalman's Reflections

A personal celebration of semaphore signalling

Adrian Vaughan

Silver Link Publishing

In Memory of the Real Railway —
An affectionate dedication
To encourage those too young to have known it
And to delight those too old to forget it.

© Adrian Vaughan 1990

*All rights reserved. No part of this publication may be reproduced,
stored in a retrieval system or transmitted, in any form or by any
means, electronic, mechanical, photocopying, recording or otherwise,
without prior permission in writing from Silver Link Publishing Ltd.*

First published in 1990
Reprinted 1992
Reprinted with revisions 1995
Paperback edition first published 2004

British Library Cataloguing in Publication Data

A catalogue record for this book is available
from the British Library.

ISBN 1 85794 239 6

Silver Link Publishing Ltd
The Trundle
Ringstead Road
Great Addington
Kettering
Northants NN14 4BW

Tel/Fax: 01536 330588
email: sales@nostalgiacollection.com
Website: www.nostalgiacollection.com

Printed and bound in Great Britain

CONTENTS

Half-title page **The most dramatic feature of a signal box was its 'frame' of levers standing in a multi-coloured rank. Signalmen kept the steel handles silver-bright by rubbing them with emery cloth or a piece of what can only be described as 'chain mail' on a leather backing. On the Great Western, a soft cloth with a blue and red lined pattern and the letters 'GWR' woven into it was used to pull the levers, not simply to avoid salty sweat rusting the bright steel but also to avoid calluses on the hands and to make pulling easier. The 'lever duster' retained its design for many years into BR(WR) days and was always considered to be the 'badge of office' of the signalman who wore it over his shoulder or tucked by one corner into the right-hand pocket of his trousers. These GWR signal levers and signal wire adjuster were in my box at Hinksey South, Oxford. No 72, the yellow up main distant signal, is nearest the camera, followed by four red home signals, Nos 71-68. The wire adjuster is fitted to the distant signal wire alone, that signal being 1,002 yards from the box and its wire being subject to considerable expansion and contraction. The handle which turns the screw adjuster lifts off to be applied to other adjusters in the box. Photographed in 1973.**

Title page **The rural idyll. Knighton Crossing signal box, almost certainly dating from 1874 and extended by one window in 1904, stood at the 69th milepost from Paddington where the railroad to Bristol was crossed by the parish lane to Longcot and Shrivenham. The great ridge of the Berkshire Downs rises to nearly 900 feet behind, along which that most ancient of roads, the Ridgeway, makes its rutted way, lonely and high above the Vale. The highest point of the ridge is crowned with an Iron Age ring fort — Uffington Castle (after which no locomotive was named) — and the side of the great hill is carved with the Iron Age fertility symbol of the White Horse which gives the Berkshire Vale its name. From 'White Horse Hill' one could follow the progress of a steam train from Steventon to Swindon. The gates and signal box were replaced by automatic half-barriers in November 1966 and these were replaced by a bridge under the line about 15 years later — something for which the land had been purchased 100 years before. Photographed in 1958. (H.O. Vaughan)**

Tell me where is fancy bred.
Or in the heart or in the head?
William Shakespeare

The rural idyll. Havenhouse in Lincolnshire from the lane, apparently very little changed since the line was doubled as far as bracing Skegness in May 1901, just in time for that year's holiday season. One expects to see a pony and trap appear at any moment, yet this photograph was taken in June 1984. This archetypal English–Victorian scene was destroyed in March 1989 by Lincolnshire County Council when the Highways Department replaced the gates with automatic half-barriers and their attendant ugliness of flimsy signs, garish colours and colour-light signals. At an LCC Highways Department exhibition on 'Improving the Environment', photographs of 'before' and 'after' were displayed under the general heading of 'How we are improving your environment'. This displays a monumental lack of feeling quite unlike the sympathy of the nineteenth century railway engineers.

INTRODUCTION AND ACKNOWLEDGEMENTS

This book is a personal view of what it was I liked about railways. I want to show the variety of railway signalling equipment from whence sprang a large part of the individuality and atmosphere of any given railway — which in part prompted the affection we had for it. My nostalgia is unashamed and unapologised for because the semaphore-operated railway, its delightful staff of men and women and all its works, was an important part of my growing up and for 15 years it was my life's work.

Now my life's work is making as accurate a record of those days as I can, and this accurate record is supposed to convey not merely facts and figures but also feelings and atmosphere. The steam railway was not run by machines but by men and women who had strong feelings of loyalty to their mates, to their engine, their station or signal box, and even to the company — especially if they worked close to some 'foreign' company. There was, in a word, a 'team spirit'. Best then if I try to record that very important spirit along with the technicalities, because that was what the steam railway was, a combination of hard technicality and strong human emotions. That is how the workpeople managed to cope with what could be described as a very difficult job. That spirit rose above the difficulties and made the job worth doing — but, and it must not be forgotten, it was the difficulties that created the team spirit.

The signal boxes have largely been swept away — and, in my opinion, the spirit with them. Unthinking, ignorant people, those with no soul, denigrate the old signalling because they think it at least 'quaint' or even inefficient alongside automatic, colour-light signals. They say 'It is 70 years old' or '100 years old' as if age is enough to condemn it — in which case we ought to pull down Norwich Cathedral and build a large Portacabin for a place of worship. Semaphore signals and their signal boxes might well be '70 years old', but they are maintained on a daily basis and for the most part require only a drop of oil now and then. They are electrically and mechanically locked as well as any colour-light and with this 'quaint' and 'inefficient' system the vast traffic of the past was carried, to a greater density than exists today.

It is also worth remembering that no signal of any kind is proof against human frailty and that the devastating accidents at Clapham Junction and Colwich, at Reading and Stafford took place under 'state of the art' modern signalling. The money was spent, the much derided semaphores and the jobs that went with them were lost, 'efficiency' had been purchased — the *Daily Blurb* assured us — but the accidents happened just the same.

When I was a signalman I gave the job my best efforts whilst enjoying the scene, the company of my mates and the work itself. Now that I am writing about those days I have to do my level best to get the facts right, and the information given has come either from my own certain knowledge or from several railway historians, expert researchers in their field, or from signalmen who worked at the place in the illustration. I am deeply indebted and wish to record my grateful thanks to David Collins, Mike Christensen, Larry Crosier, Martin Elms, Reg Instone, John Morris, Roger Newman, Jerry Plane, George Pryer and Garth Tilt. Other experts consulted were Richard Adderson, Dr Robert Preston Hendry and his son Robert Powell Hendry, Dr Jack Hollick, John Miller, Peter Punchard and Robert Skoulding (signalman — retired — at Reedham Junction).

I must also thank those fellow railway lovers who have written to me over the years with their recollections of those happy, railway, days and who have allowed me to draw upon their memories. Where possible I have checked their remembrances and found them to be correct, while the spirit they wrote of I know existed since I enjoyed it myself. These people are: Don Attwood on Midgham; Mrs Gladys Carter on Melton Constable and Langor

Bridge signal box; Mr Raymond Meek; the late Inspector Percy Youngman; Mrs Phyllis Youngman on Melton Constable and the M&GNJR; Locomotive Inspector Jack Gardener on Ledbury tunnel; Traffic Inspector Alan Johnson on the GWR 'New Line'; Signalwoman Doreen Spackman on the wartime GWR; Michael Sadler on Thingley Junction; Ray Thomas on Chippenham; and John Whiting on Kington and Leominster. I should also like to thank Brian Jackson, Kenneth Leech, Mike Christensen, John Morris and Dr Ian Scrimgeour, Ray Thomas, Doreen Spackman, Mrs Phyllis Youngman and Mrs Gladys Carter for supplying photographs. Uncredited photographs were taken by the author.

Written sources consulted in my research were: *The Signal Box*, Signalling Study Group; *Over Shap to Carlisle*, Harold Bowtell; *British Main Line Gradient Profiles*, published by Ian Allan; *The History of the Great Western Railway* Vols 1 and 2, E.T. McDermott; *History of the Southern Railway*, Dendy-Marshal/Kidner; *Railways of the Southern Region*, Geoffrey Body; *The Midland & South Western Junction Railway*, Vol 1, David Bartholemew; *Outline of Irish Railway History*, H.C. Casserley; *Irish Railways since 1916*, Michael H.C. Baker; *An Account of the Signalling of the SMJ*, M. Christensen (privately circulated); *A Pictorial Record of LNWR Signalling*, Richard Foster; Ordnance Survey, 6th edition, 1 inch maps; GWR Service Time Tables 1936; GWR Sectional Appendices to Service Time Tables; *The Great Western Railway* (GWR 'Private' publication, 1926); BR(WR) Service Time Tables 1954.

Anyone wishing to know more about all kinds of signalling systems should join the Signalling Record Society; the address of the Membership Secretary is Gribdae Cottage, Kirkcudbright DG6 4QD.

Adrian Vaughan
Barney
Norfolk

An ancient fireplace, from the days when signalmen worked 12 hours a day as a matter of routine and needed somewhere to cook or re-heat food. This box is well provided for with two teapots in case there should be a large influx of visitors, permanent way men for instance — the tea must always flow. The signalman's chair was often a good advertisement for human inventiveness and initiative. Its genesis unknown, it was usually broken down, ingeniously mended, covered with some exceedingly doubtful cushions — and very comfortable. On the wall are some telephones and the booking desk carrying the train register with 'extra train notices' hanging at eye level. The lockers will provide seating for the tea-swilling visitors. Ballingrane Junction, Co Limerick, 1980.

SIGNALMAN'S REFLECTIONS

A LIFE ON THE M&GN

Being a signalman was probably the best job on the railway. It was clean, comfortable, responsible, and with a perfect view of the finest free show on earth — the regular passage of steam-hauled trains. The wages could have been higher and most men in the lower grades — usually those who had growing families and therefore needed extra money — had to struggle. In the large towns where there was heavy industry which paid higher wages, some railwaymen left the service out of necessity, but many remained, preferring the more pleasant working environment of the railway. In the countryside, however, too far from the 'dark satanic mills' of industry, the men could not have changed jobs even if they had wanted to, which is why so many signalmen and railwaymen generally kept a good garden. The relatively low wages were not that much of a bar to a pleasant life.

If a man had a country signal box he had the additional pleasure of the landscape, farm animals and assorted wildlife. It was also a job for life, but so was any job on the 'steam railway'. The pre-nationalisation railway companies and the steam-era British Railways provided secure employment for whole families. Whilst the 'Great' companies had their fair share of family connections, the ultimate in the 'family railway' stakes were the smaller lines such as the Somerset & Dorset and the Eastern & Midlands Railway; the latter became the Midland & Great Northern Joint in 1893. Arthur Carter, the son of an M&GN man, worked for 38 years at Langor Bridge box on the M&GN, a couple of miles east of Fakenham. The signal box was at the bottom of his garden, so close that his wife Gladys in the kitchen could hear the bells ringing and the thud of the levers as Albert 'pulled off' for a train. He was a quiet countryman with the utterly laudable ambition to remain where he was, serving the public faithfully in what appeared to be, in the eyes of the foolish world, a very humble capacity.

Every day for 38 years, barring rest days and holidays, Albert walked down his garden path, through a little gate in the railway fence and up into the box. The M&GN experienced many seasonal peaks of intense traffic through the year, particularly sugar beet, the Scottish women who came by the train-load to gut herrings for a living at Yarmouth and Lowestoft, and the holidaymakers from the Midlands and the North of England. At these peak times, when the passenger trains were 'queued up block 'n' block', Arthur Carter would have one train struggling eastwards up Barney bank between his post and Thursford, and another waiting at his home signal, just west of the Fakenham main road. These old trains were made up of some very motley coaches, without corridors and therefore without toilets, and the compartments frequently contained some very uncomfortable people, especially children. Parents would appeal to the train's guard, he would appeal to Gladys, and many were the occasions when the wretched travellers were welcomed into her home so they could use her lavatory while the train waited at the signal.

Gladys was born in 1900 at that little Derby in the heart of Norfolk, Melton Constable, where her father, Tom Riches, was an engine driver. She spoke with affection about the railway 'family' but she also spoke honestly and showed that, like all families, matters did not always run sweetly. Her earliest memories are of the railway pervading her life — and indeed the life of the whole of that

Gladys Carter's father, Tom Riches, with his beautiful M&GN 'C' Class 4-4-0 at Cromer, *circa* 1900. Note the Whittaker tablet snatcher bolted on to the tender side. (*Courtesy Gladys Carter*)

railway town. She was often woken at 2 am by the sound of the call boy 'knocking up' her father for duty, and at 7 am she would wake again and hurry down to the kitchen to find the ha'penny her dad had hidden for her, in a screw of paper, somewhere in the room. When he was on nights, Gladys did not see her father for a week.

Melton Constable owed its existence to the Midland & Great Northern Joint. The locomotive works, the engine shed and the station dominated the town, with William Marriott as Engineer, Locomotive Superintendent and, later, Traffic Manager as well in charge of everything. He had supervised the construction of much of the mileage which finally formed the Eastern & Midland and M&GN and so he *was* the M&GN and dominated the life of every person in Melton Constable. He was a very good manager and a fine locomotive man and was consequently highly respected by all the workers; but he was also a man of missionary zeal and did his utmost to foist his particular brand of hellfire and brimstone upon every man, woman and child in the town.

There was a divide in Melton between Marriott and those who liked — or knuckled under to — his form of paternalistic authoritarianism, and those who did their best to retain their own opinions. His demands for strict temperance and bible study amongst his employees led to hypocrisy amongst some bible-thumping train crews. Marriott's 'Institute', a large building which served as a technical college and coffee house, provided railwaymen with tea for a penny and a bath for tuppence — but no alcohol. Railwaymen who wished to progress their careers on the M&GN did not dare to be seen going into the Hastings Arms, opposite Melton Constable station, but would make up for lost time in the pubs at Yarmouth which they considered far enough away from Melton to be out of reach of Marriott's missionary zeal.

Gladys Carter's father, Tom Riches, was of an independent frame of mind and was not on Marriott's list of 'the Saved'. Tom volunteered for the First World War and on his return to Melton Constable Marriott refused to take him back owing to his 'irreligious habits' — as defined by Marriott. However, for once there was a law above that of Mr William Marriott and Mr Riches was taken on again as a driver. In fairness to a remarkable man, it must be said that Marriott was always very concerned for the welfare of 'his' people — he just took his concern too far in some respects. One instance, among many, of his caring attitude was when Gladys's mother was taken critically ill at the end of her pregnancy; Marriott at once ordered a one-coach special to dash her down to Norwich City station for the Norfolk & Norwich hospital.

A name almost as famous as Marriott on the M&GN was Youngman. More than one Youngman family worked on the line, but here I am referring to Percy Youngman's family. Three generations of his family helped to build, to run and eventually to close the M&GN. Grandfather Youngman was a farm worker near Corpusty (pronounced 'Corpstee') when the Lynn & Fakenham Railway began construction in 1881. He was taken on as a navvy and when the line was opened through Corpusty the following year he was employed as Ganger for track maintenance. He got his son John into employment on the E&MR — as the Lynn & Fakenham had by then become — in 1889 as a messenger lad at Corpusty. John was a bright lad who became a porter at Aylsham, booking clerk at Norwich City station and Station Master at Gayton

Percy Youngman's grandfather, Ganger Youngman (left) with the porter, Station Master and 'PC Plod' at Corpusty & Saxthorpe station. (*Courtesy Phyllis Youngman*)

Station Master Youngman, Percy's father, with Percy's little sister and some of his staff at Gayton Road station in about 1905. (*Courtesy Phyllis Youngman*)

Road where Percy was born on 13 June 1907.

John Youngman was very, very keen on railway work and passed on his enthusiasm to Percy. He gave his son a very much cut down shunting pole and the little lad carried it proudly as he accompanied his father 'round the estate', as they, like many railwaymen, sarcastically called the daily perambulation of the sidings forming the shunting yard of the wayside station. Gayton Road took in coal and exported bricks and sand from nearby Bawsey. The bricks were loaded carefully, sandwiched between layers of straw, into open wagons and labelled for all over Britain, but the sand was sent to a glass works in Cheshire in 'private owner' wagons which carried the company name in bold letters — 'JOSEPH BOAM'. As at many country stations, the Gayton Road staff received Christmas presents from satisfied passengers and traders, and among the hampers that arrived from the large houses round about was one conveying Melton Mowbray pies for the staff, with the compliments of Joseph Boam Ltd.

There was always plenty of traffic in the yard — empty and loaded wagons to be shunted, plenty to do. Starting from the earliest age in this happily industrious atmosphere, Percy grew up enjoying hard work and the feeling of being busy and useful.

In those days telephones on the railway were almost or completely unknown, and messages were passed by the 'single-needle' telegraph instrument. This was a visual system of Morse code used to transmit messages by electricity. An instrument had a single centre-pivoted needle which was deflected to the left or the right by an electro-magnet. The man who was transmitting the message moved a handle to the left or right to deflect the needle of the instrument at the opposite end of the wire. The needle snapped over smartly against a little 'stop' made of wire, so each deflection was marked by a slight 'tink' sound as the steel needle hit the stop. The railwaymen were supposed to watch the needle and read off the words as they were spelt out — a deflection left and right, for example, was 'A'.

It was a tedious, cumbersome business, since several instruments were all on one circuit, and the men required the knowledge of an intricate procedure. It would have been even more cumbersome had not the railway company used many code words to stand for whole sentences, and

had not the railwaymen turned the system into true Morse by unofficially using the *sound* made by the needle hitting its wire stops to read off the message. Sometimes the men fitted the wire stops with tiny 'sounders' so that they could better differentiate between a 'left' and a 'right' deflection. They could then look down at their message pad and write out the message without looking at the needle. The system required of its operators the utmost skill and a deep knowledge of the system, and Percy Youngman was put to learning it by his father at the age of 8.

To start off, his father placed two jam-jars on the kitchen table, one full — for the right deflection — and one half empty — for the left deflection — and with a pencil he tapped out the letter codes. Later on he obtained a 'teaching instrument' which sat on the kitchen table. This was simply a mock-up with two faces and two handles, back to back. Percy sat on one side with his Dad on the other side; the needles were manipulated and the routines learned. When an operator was truly proficient he would, having answered his call letter, send 'G', which meant 'Go on', whereupon the sender would rattle off the whole message without any hesitation. Percy was ten when he was able to give 'G' to his Dad on the teaching instrument.

By that time his father had been promoted to Weybourne station. Percy took the keenest interest in railway work and really enjoyed life there. He was ten, well versed in the ways of rural railways and competent in that most difficult and intricate of all railway operations — the 'single needle'. Apart from railway matters he also took a keen interest in fishing and gardening. The Great War was raging, food was short and railwaymen were encouraged to cultivate the lineside. Percy had a regular farm on the trackside bank at Weybourne with ducks, chickens, pigs, a goat and — for a time — even a horse, all in his father's name, of course. Down on the shingle beach he caught horse mackerel which came leaping on to the beach in their shoals, jumping out of the water like dolphins and stranding themselves on the black pebbles. Amongst them were little whitebait. He collected and sold the fish along with eggs from his ducks and chickens.

Twice a week a train of municipal rubbish was sent from Sheringham for dumping in a pit near the railway at Weybourne. The train was unloaded by contractors who gave young Percy a few coppers when he assisted in the work. He helped to cart and bury hundreds and hundreds of ginger-beer bottles — the kind with a marble in the neck for a seal. Rubbish they were in 1917, but in 1972 Percy recalled them and, realising that times had changed, alerted the North Norfolk Railway to the treasure trove under what appeared to be a grassy field. Percy helped to dig them up and the NNR sold each bottle for £1.50. In 1917 there was a penny back on returned bottles — so much for inflation! The site of the rubbish tip is now covered by the NNR's workshop at Weybourne.

The railwaymen from Weybourne to Lowestoft saw a good deal of the War when warships patrolled and sometimes fought along the coast, when the Germans bombarded Yarmouth from the sea, and when the first bombs to fall on England exploded on Sheringham, having been dropped from a Zeppelin. Percy was sitting 'in the little house' — on the loo — at the bottom of the garden on this particular day. The loo, by the way, was a very smart one with a water flush system to a septic tank — a matter of good fortune for the Youngmans, who thus did not have to empty a 'thunderbox', but equally a matter of some disgust for the local permanent way gang whose job it was to empty the septic tank.

Percy was sitting on 'the throne', the door open, admiring the view over the fields to the windmill and the sea, when he heard the strangest noise he had ever heard in all his ten years. It was a rapid, roaring, hammering sound which quite frightened the boy, sitting there bolt upright. Then, appearing slowly from the left, came a long, white cigar-shaped object as strange as a 'flying saucer', floating along accompanied by the awful noise. He dragged up his pants and rushed up the garden and indoors to his mother. The Thing droned inland and dropped some bombs on Bayfield Hall, where there was a tented camp occupied by a Highland Regiment, killing a few men. This was a Zeppelin, and the twentieth century had arrived in North Norfolk.

Weybourne station saw a great many troop movements, fit soldiers going out, the maimed coming home. Ambulance trains disgorged their tragic loads on to the platform and into the yard, and Percy vividly recalled walking past the rows of stretchers, placed side by side as close as sardines in a can, the men white-faced in the lamplight, limbs bound in bloody bandages, their drab uniforms bloody and still covered in the Flanders mud. It was the most terrible sight and one which still affected Percy in 1982. He helped with the stretchers and he helped load troop trains. Army mules and troopers' horses were packed into ordinary cattle trucks as tight as could be, but the officers' horses — 'chargers', not 'horses', Percy would be quick to correct me — went in proper horse-boxes in peacetime comfort. The continuing, terrible War would not bring about the collapse of civilisation, but the abandonment of class distinctions, even for horses, would.

Percy did well at school and passed the entrance examinations for the Post Office and the Police; he was actually attracted to a career in the latter. When his father heard this, there was a terrible row in which the whole family joined — with grandad coming over by train from Corpusty. Percy had been trained from a baby to be an M&GN man — he was betrothed and had no say in the matter. His father wanted him to enter the railway clerical grades but there were no vacancies, so they made him a Lad Porter at Weybourne under his father and he commenced his (paid) railway service in 1923, aged 16.

Considering the economic chaos and social strife following the Great War he was lucky to get a job at all on the M&GN which, even in the halcyon days before 1914, had been a 'shoestring' concern, short of money and always looking out for ways of cutting costs. Percy was a fine, tall man with a very strict sense of duty — although he enjoyed some fun in the practical joking which was part of railway life — and he might well have had a more prosperous career in the Police, but his was a *railway* family so there was no point in wondering. He was moved to a portering job at Lenwade, on the Melton Constable–Norwich City line, in 1924, and there he stuck for nine years until, in 1933, he was offered his first promotion — to a God-forsaken agricultural station, remote in the vastness of the Fens, which rejoiced in the singular name of 'Counter Drain'. The following year he became a 'Relief Porter', which on the M&GN meant he was expected to do absolutely any job but drive or fire locomotives — and to carry out these duties at any station from Bourne to Lowestoft and Cromer. There was little specialisation on the M&GN; a railwayman was expected to be adept at everything from station accounts to shunting and signalling.

His life then was nothing but travelling, working and sleeping in 'lodges', some of which were good and some of which were completely appalling. When he was acting as 'Porter-guard' out of Yarmouth, he lodged at a house in Wells Street where the housewife had no knowledge at all of cooking. Percy lived on sprats, bloaters and kippers. One Christmas she put the celebratory chicken in the oven with the guts still inside. One would have thought he would have found more congenial lodgings, but maybe that would not have been so simple in Yarmouth in 1935; anyhow, Percy continued to use the lodge and to suffer the food. It seems likely, in fact, that the lady was trying to tell him something, because one day he came down to eat and found a large pile of very wet, very soiled and very smelly nappies on the chair he used. He

Percy Youngman as an LNER guard at Great Yarmouth in 1935. He was working the 'Tantivy' steam railcar at this period. (*Courtesy Phyllis Youngman*)

finally recognised this very heavy hint and found other lodgings.

During his time as acting Porter-guard he worked the 'Tantivy' steam railcar, the 'Fisher-girl' specials, where every woman carried a razor-sharp gutting knife, excursions for holidaymakers, goods and regular passenger trains. There were occasions in the summer when he was 'relieving' the Station Master or a signalman at Lenwade or Drayton and would be put on as a guard for a week or two, based at Norwich City. Then he had a ten-mile cycle ride in the dark to the station to pick up his train — 'ten GNs and a restaurant car' — through to Skegness and back, looking after ticket examination, taking in and giving out railway internal mail and looking out for signals *en route*; then at the end of a seemingly endless day, he would cycle ten miles home to his lodging. Properly he would have been relieved at South Lynn and the furthest west a Norwich man would have gone — the extreme limit of his official road knowledge — was Sutton Bridge, but M&GN men were bred to take on anything and as a result they would go just about anywhere they were asked — and that without a 'Pilotman' too!

In 1936 he was working as guard on a train to Norwich City. He examined tickets and made sure he spotted the distant signal for each signal box — 'because the guard's in charge of the train'. They had a 'Queen Mary' on the front, a big, ex-Great Central Railway express loco, and were clipping along very smartly. Speed increased down Whitwell bank and when Percy saw that Whitwell & Reepham's distant signal was 'off' he thought this was too much encouragement for the driver; there was a turn-out through the platform loop at the station ahead and Percy wondered if the driver had forgotten. 'I don't know, Pat,' he thought to himself, 'but you're hopping along too smart for me.' He hurried back to his van and 'put the setter in' — applied the vacuum brake — because the guard, not the driver, is in charge of the train.

During the Second World War Percy was a signalman at various places on the M&GN and recalled seeing a Great Western and also a Southern Railway engine on troop trains at various times, although he did not recognise the classes. He was close by when Weybourne camp and Sheringham town were attacked from the air. The bombs on Weybourne camp came down with a terrifying, whistling scream causing Percy, who was cycling to work, to make a perfect, arching dive from his bike to the nearest ditch without so much as a conscious thought. He was at Melton when the Germans machine-gunned the Locomotive Works' water towers, killing the Works Foreman, Mr English. When working at Runton Junctions he had grandstand views of duels between the Luftwaffe and the Royal Navy. The Yarmouth–Sheringham area was 'bomb alley' — East Anglia was so close to France and so full of military bases that civilians saw a great deal of the war.

As signalman at Massingham he controlled access to a huge underground store of aviation fuel which lay 1½ miles west of the village towards Hillington. A siding leading to the store was connected to the main line by a set of points which could be moved by the guard of the train after Percy had electrically released the ground frame lever. The store still exists at the side of the main road but a 'luxury dogotel' stands astride Percy's beloved M&GN. One day, two British fighter planes collided in mid-air and went down in flames on top — as far as Percy could tell — of the petrol store. He had given permission for a petrol train to come from Hillington and it had passed beyond Hillington's signals when the mid-air collision occurred. Percy at once telephoned the lady crossing-keeper at No 7 crossing — whose house is in use today as an ordinary dwelling close to the 'dogotel' — and ordered her to place three detonators on the line a mile back from her house and stand by them with a red flag, 'and if you haven't got a flag wave your knickers!' She stopped the petrol train — with or without her knickers, Percy did not know.

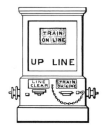

WOMEN RAILWAY WORKERS

There were thousands of men like Percy who gave their all to the railway, and indeed there were thousands of women who would have done likewise had they been given the opportunity. During the two World Wars women came into just about any grade but engine driver and fireman, and did at least as good, if not better, a job than the men. Many of the women would have been glad to continue their service because they enjoyed the sense of public service, the responsibility, the comradeship and, doubtless, the extra attraction for women of being independent, of earning their own wage and of being released from the kitchen sink — although whether cleaning engines or carriages was a fair exchange for the kitchen sink is open to question. However, being a porteress and going on to become a signalwoman certainly was a pleasant job which very few women were allowed to keep once the war was over.

Doreen Spackman and her friend Thelma Hoare, of Burbage, Wiltshire, were 18 when the Second World War began. They volunteered for railway work and were posted, not to their local station, Savernake, but to Steventon where Mr Ellis was Station Master. The girls were thrilled with the new-found feeling of freedom, of being away from the village, of doing a really useful job of work, of receiving a pay packet and of being independent. But for the war they would have had to stay at home until they married — and then they would still have been at home in Burbage. They enjoyed portering, especially shunting with the 'fly' goods, riding on the engine and larking with the locomen. Mr Ellis tried to keep a very fatherly eye on them and would come down the yard calling 'Miss Spackman, Miss Hoare' if the buffers stopped clanging and all went quiet. He had not seen women working on the railway since the First World War and did not quite know how to approach the girls, remaining rather formal, out of shyness.

Doreen and Thelma were inseparable buddies and in 1942 became signalwomen at Collingbourne Ducis on the old Midland & South Western Junction Railway section of the GWR, where old Mr Marquiss was Station Master. They learned the job in the normal way, by watching and doing and reading the rule books in the evening until they could satisfy the Chief Inspector of the Bristol Division of their competence.

Signalling was really what they enjoyed and they had a wonderful time. In 1944 Doreen took the correspondence course on the Rules & Regulations, just for fun, and passed the written examination. The letter advising her of her success came in an envelope embossed on the back with GREAT WESTERN RAILWAY COMPANY and carrying on the front the printed legend: 'DISEASES OF ANIMALS CIRCULARS — IMMEDIATE'. I have it here beside me as I write. Whether the choice of envelope was made deliberately by some jealous, male, clerk we will never know. At the bottom of the official letter, which I also have here, Mr Marquiss has written, in superb 1880s copperplate, 'Hearty congratulations'.

The M&SW, which since 1923 had been a neglected, historical curiosity, cut north-south from the LMS at Cheltenham, to the Southern Railway at Andover, crossing GWR territory and the military area of Salisbury Plain. It was full of ancient, non-GWR equipment and signals and was up-dated for the war because of its vital strategic importance in connecting Birmingham and the North with Southampton.

Tanks, aircraft, bombs, ammunition, ambulance and troop trains thronged the tracks giving Doreen and Thelma a lot of work. As she told me: 'I suppose it is wrong to say so, but we did enjoy ourselves during the War . . . there was such a lot to do and such good feeling between us all.' Comradeship was the order of the day — 'get stuck in' and keep the job moving — especially during the War when everyone was pulling together for victory. Ceremony was not stood upon.

★   ★   ★

On the morning of 22 September 1944, Signalwoman Alice Hutchinson was on duty in the new signal box at Whitchurch (Hants) — or 'Whitchurch Aunts' as the porter used to call out when trains stopped there, in case anyone should think they were at Whitchurch in Shropshire. This Whitchurch was on that other lonely, north–south railway which became one of *the* strategic railways in Britain between 1939 and 1945 — the Didcot, Newbury & Southampton line.

Between Newbury and Shawford Junction it was a single track railway with crossing loops, and one such crossing place was at Whitchurch. Alice had the 5 am Eastleigh–Alexandra Dock Government Stores train, 54 wagons and a brake-van, on the up loop, and as the 7.5 am Winchester to Reading passenger train was following she told the driver and guard of the freight to draw forward clear of No 7 points, and then to set back on to the down loop. This they did, the Winchester passenger passed by and the freight had then to be replaced on the up loop to make way for the down, 7.45 am Newbury to Winchester passenger.

The goods drew ahead until the brake-van was clear of No 7 points whereupon Alice set them normal — they were worked by electric motor through a short lever in the signal box — and then reversed points 11, also worked by motor. Unfortunately she forgot to pull short lever 10 to complete the setting up of the route. As a result she could not lower ground disc No 8 because its lever was held by the mechanical interlocking. The down 'stopper' was waiting to come from Litchfield, and time was short. Alice saw nothing wrong, no indicators were 'dangling', all was in order, so as she could not work No 8 she waved No 26 up and down as a signal to the guard to bring his train back. Eager to be of assistance, Guard Rouse, a Didcot man, waved his train back without checking to make sure the road was set. Of course it was not, and with much clattering, banging and crashing his brake-van and four wagons were derailed at No 10 points — although the brake-van, a gentlemanly Great Western 'TOAD' No 17428, most obligingly

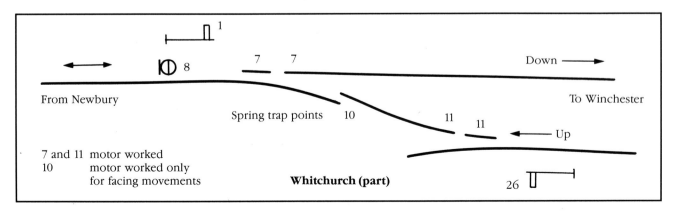

From Newbury   To Winchester

Spring trap points   10   11   11   ← Up

7 and 11   motor worked
10   motor worked only
            for facing movements

Whitchurch (part)   26

re-railed itself at once — but the four vans were LMS and sullenly refused to co-operate.

The line was completely blocked and buses were at once laid on to take the passengers off the 7.45 am Newbury, waiting at Litchfield, and to cover other disrupted train services. The front part of the goods train, 48 wagons, was, meanwhile, hauled through to Litchfield, the guard riding on the last wagon, where another brake-van was waiting. This was attached and the train left at 11.40. The breakdown vans, ordered from Reading at 9.40 am, arrived at the lonely spot at 11.25 am. One wagon was re-railed by noon, clearing the down line, and the up line was clear by 2.15 pm.

SMALL LAYOUT — BIG TROUBLE

These lonely little stations were surprisingly busy, even without the odd derailment. The layout at Wrangaton, the station for a pub and a few houses high on the shoulder of Dartmoor, drew to itself some very busy shunting at certain times of the day. The line ran through a sharply curved cutting and fell steeply in each direction, factors which made shunting work even more difficult for all the staff concerned.

Signalman Hawke was on duty in the 1890-vintage signal box, set back into the cutting side below the road bridge, on the dismal, winter morning of 8 November 1947. With him he had the station porter, Charlie Clark, who was to direct shunting operations when the 5.45 am Plymouth Laira–Hackney (Newton Abbot) pick-up goods arrived. There was an empty coal wagon — a 'pool' — in the coal siding on the down side and seven loaded open wagons on the cattle dock road, also on the down side of the line, all to be taken to Monksmoor depot adjacent to the up refuge. The seven wagons were standing handily at the London end of the siding. Three loaded cattle trucks were at the Plymouth end. These were two large and one small LNER 'Oxfits' containing 18 cattle consigned from Ashburton to Wrangaton the previous afternoon.

The pick-up goods arrived at 7.15 am hauled by 4-6-0 No 5011 *Tintagel Castle*. Dawn had only just broken, the morning was still dark and the oil lamps in the signal box and the one on the engine still glowed bright yellow. The engine's fire was bright orange, reflecting off polished metal as the engine hissed past the signal box, drawing its train clear of the up refuge points.

When the train had been deposited in the latter siding, the engine came forward and stopped opposite the signal box in order to reverse to the coal siding via points 8/6 to hook on to the empty 'pool'. Having coupled this against the tender it drew back over the crossover. What ought then to have happened, in hindsight, is that the engine should have continued along the up main beyond

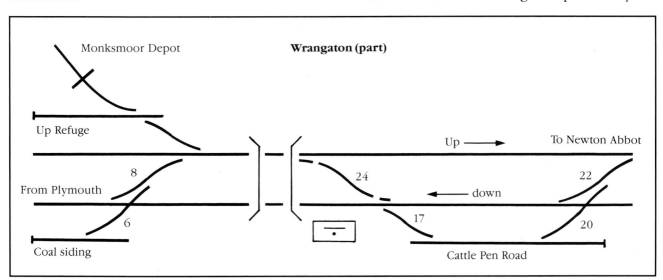

Monksmoor Depot   **Wrangaton (part)**

Up Refuge

Up ⟶   To Newton Abbot

8   24

From Plymouth   down   22

6   17   20

Coal siding   Cattle Pen Road

points 22/20. These would have been reversed and the engine would have backed down into the cattle pen road, picked up the seven loaded wagons, drawn them back to the up main and then set back to the up refuge and coupled them to the train.

What was actually decided on that dark, windy, winter morning was to pick up the empty 'pool' through points 8/6, go back to the up side so that point 6 could be reversed, then back to the down main through point 8, and from there to the cattle pen road, via points 17. Here they hooked on to the three cattle wagons and, believing that the seven open wagons beyond were coupled to them, drew back out to the down main. The idea was to leave the 'opens' between points 24 and 22, push the cattle trucks back into the siding, then run round the 'opens' via the up main — points 24 and 22 — hook on to them, draw them to the up side and set them back on to the train in the up refuge. A more clumsy and amateurish way of going about the job could hardly be imagined and it is no surprise to learn that the porter was an inexperienced, temporary employee.

Neither Charlie nor the train guard checked that all the wagons were coupled and of course it was soon discovered that the 'opens' were not attached to the 'Oxfits'. The guard therefore let off the brake to gravitate them out of the siding. Unfortunately gravity took over, the wagons got away from the guard and collided violently with the cattle wagons. All three 'Oxfits' were derailed and one was overturned, killing two bullocks. Three of the loaded open wagons were derailed. The time was 7.37 am.

As the beasts bellowed, plunged and kicked in their terror in the smashed 'Oxfits', Signalman Hawke telephoned for the breakdown vans while the others tried to clear the up main. The wagons were fouling it, but not by much, and by dint of hard work the men on the spot managed to force the wagons sufficiently far to permit a bare clearance, and single line working was instituted between Ivybridge and Brent at 8.50 am.

The route was an exceptionally busy one and at once there was terrific disruption of traffic. Thirteen expresses and two or three stopping trains were delayed by up to 93 minutes. Three more local trains were cancelled and one express was

The signal box at Wrangaton, with the remains of the cattle pens and an empty space where the siding was, looking towards Newton Abbot from the bridge, *circa* 1959. (*Peter Barlow/Author's Collection*)

terminated at Newton Abbot and the passengers taken on by bus. Four expresses went by the Southern route and one, the 9.45 am Penzance–Paddington, suffered extra delay since it was conveying a full-width GWR dining car, No 9509, which could not go via Crediton and so had to be shunted out of the train at Plymouth North Road. Five freight trains were cancelled or badly delayed and South Devon/Cornish freight further east was held in yards at Bristol and Taunton.

The vans and crane arrived at 10.30 and took possession of the up main from 11.30 to 12.55 — causing a complete blockade — to enable the crane to lift the wagons on to the track. A short length of damaged track had to be re-laid and signal fittings replaced, and normal working was resumed at 3.20 pm. A bill for £5 16s 7d (£5.83p) was sent to the Ashburton farmer, Mr Hillson, for the conveyance of his cattle.

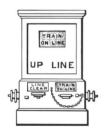

RAILWAY PRIDE

The manually-operated railway attracted hard-working, loyal people who found fulfilment in the job, not merely a wage. It is a paradox of human nature that work which could be described in terms of hardship and general unpleasantness could simultaneously be congenial to good-hearted people who simply wished to work and to serve. One might point to the 'anti-social hours', relatively low pay, the loneliness of the signal box or the lack of a lavatory or running water, the dirt and heat of locomotive work, but it seems to me, having done the job for many years, that all this was a challenge to be overcome and that the advantages to one's self-esteem and feelings of fellowship with one's workmates far outweighed these merely material disadvantages.

All over the railway there were examples of the spirit which prevailed. Take for instance Chester station which was under joint GWR/LMS manage-ment. The signalling was LNWR but the station was a 'Joint' one and all staff buttons bore the legend 'GWR-LMS'. Here in the '30s Oxford's No 4021 *British Monarch* would bring in an express from Paddington, or Chester's No 2903 *Lady of Lyons* would go out on the 10.15 Birkenhead to Paddington beneath LNWR signal gantries, passing old LNWR 'Claughton' or 'Precedent' Classes and sometimes even the mighty LMS 'Coronation' Class 'Pacifics'. The rivalry was intense.

The GWR's 11 am Manchester to Paddington, 'Castle'-hauled, left Chester at 12.30 pm from Platform 2, and at precisely that moment, from Platform 3, the LMS started a Euston–Holyhead express hauled by a 'Princess' 'Pacific'. Both trains were to run parallel for two glorious miles to Saltney Junction where the GWR train turned away to the south. Can you imagine the excitement each day at 12.29, as railwaymen stood around the two engines, each blowing off at the safety valves, just waiting for the off? Out along the line, men and boys working at the engine sheds would be keeping an eye out to watch the contestants come blasting past, straining for the honour of their respective company.

Can you also imagine what would have happened to the signalman in Chester No 4 box if he failed to give BOTH trains the road simultaneously? It is said that on one terrible occasion the LMS engine was signalled out fraction-ally later than that of the GWR, whereupon the signalman in No 4 box was de-bagged by the LMS loyalists and hung upside down by his feet from the window of his box.

The train guards gave their 'Right away' whistles dead on time, the engines whistled — or hooted in the case of the LMS engine — and off they went, drowning the cheers from the usual gallery of locospotters. Slipping was a crime — the sanding gear levers were worked with a will — and the din was terrific. The odds were on the GWR engine winning the race but that did not prevent loyal LMS men from putting money on 'the red-'un'. It was in fact normal for the GWR train to beat the LMS, but *pax* all you LMS types, for the GWR train was always the lightest, owing to the load restriction on Gresford bank. I do not seriously suggest that a 'Castle' could out-pull a 'Princess'.

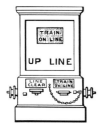

THE RAILWAY'S LOYAL PENSIONERS

Sometimes a retired railwayman living near a station would visit the porters or the signalman when he, the pensioner, was off for a pint in the Station Hotel, and almost at once his recollections would pour forth, as mellow and nostalgic as the sunset on a summer evening. Ted Shelley had been a 'top link' London guard before, during and after the Great War, and had retired to a bungalow in Midgham, Berkshire, close to the GWR main line over which he had so often worked. He was one of those men one sees in old photographs, tall and smart in his frock coat, high, stiff collar and a rose in his buttonhole — 'Aldington's Peacocks' they were called, after Charles Aldington, the GWR's General Manager from 1919 until 1921. He was always famous for his own, immaculate style of dress.

Ted had worked 'double home' from London to Neyland and Penzance as a normal part of his duty, and in the great blizzard of 27 March 1916 he had been snowbound with his train, arriving in Paddington 10 hours late after being 19 hours on the road. Ted, who before the War had recorded half-minute delays in his Train Journal, was very shocked and blamed the bad weather on the continuous concussions to the atmosphere caused by the artillery bombardments in France.

He often worked 'the Limited', 'double home Penzance'. All these trips had merged as one in his memory, the time made up, the engines and the men he had worked with from 'Stars' like *Swallow-field Park* to 'Kings' over that long, weary road in sunshine and rain, and the parcels and luggage he had shifted and stowed. But one incident stuck in his mind. He was working the down 'Limited' and had a Plymouth to Helston horse-box on behind his brake-van to be dropped off at Gwinear Road. The porter there uncoupled it. The Station Master gave 'Right' to Ted, Ted gave 'Right' to his driver and the express drew away.

Ted watched his train from the rear van as it slid past the platform, went inside and noted the departure time in his Journal. He then looked out, back to the station. The horse-box was following him down the 1 in 147 gradient — and it was steeply downhill for miles. Ted realised at once that he had better stop the wagon now before it picked up too great a momentum, so he lifted the brake setter immediately and stood by for the crash. The blow was not serious but heavy enough. Two suitcases shot off a rack in the rear coach to fall on the head of a passenger but no great harm was done. For his quick thinking Ted had a commendation written into his record and was granted as many free passes as he wanted over the following 12 months.

As a 'slip guard' he had a very serious job indeed, because when he pulled that slipping lever to detach the slip coach from the main train he effectively became the driver of a train. Like all jobs on the railway, he was expected to find out for himself how to do the job. There was no such thing as a training school for slip guards, or signalmen, or anything else, except the great 'University of Life'. No wonder the slip coaches used to run past stations occasionally. Anyhow, Ted rode with slip guards, read the book of regulations, got an idea of how to do the job, did it some more and finally became very skilful at 'knowing the road'.

Just how skilful is illustrated by what happened when he was guard of the Weymouth slip on the down 'Limited'. They left Paddington in bright sun and the weather stayed fine until they blasted over Savernake summit. But as they ran down into the Vale of Pewsey a mist thickened into a fog. After Lavington, when the train was running at a good 80 mph, the fog was dense. Edington & Bratton was a dim blur as they raced through and Ted was wrestling hard with his conscience — should he let the train go on while he slipped on the approach to Heywood Road Junction, or should he stop it to detach the coach? He did not at all like the idea of stopping the 'Cornish Riviera'. Perhaps the fog was not too bad after all and everyone would take him for a 'Wally'. He decided he would try it and took the padlock off the slipping lever. Would he stop miles short of the junction home signal or would he overshoot and go down the Westbury Avoiding Line after the express? It was a hell of a decision to have to take.

He peered forward into the murk, eyes watering in the slipstream, desperately looking for his landmarks. Whoosh! Was that it? He decided it was and yanked over the slipping lever. The hook fell away, the vacuum brake pipes parted and the slip coach brake went on. The rest of the train drew away into the gloom and after a moment he pushed the lever forward to mid-position, thus releasing the brake and allowing the coach to coast at 70 mph.

Up on the engine the driver saw the 'Train Pipe' needle dip and bob up again as the vacuum pipes were broken and air entered the system until it was thrown out by the cross-head air pump. He knew then that the slip had been made. Back on the speeding slip coach Ted was working blind, but he braked, released and braked again. He was down to 10 mph and wondering whether he was 'out in the middle of nowhere' or somewhere near his target when the red and yellow lights of Heywood Road Junction's junction signal emerged from the murk. He brought the coach to a stand right at the foot of the signal post. Almost at once he heard footsteps crunching on the ballast and a voice said: 'You judged that well, guard'. It was the permanent way man on 'fogging' duties. After that the pilot engine came out of its siding, hooked on to the coach and drew it into Westbury to be attached to the Weymouth train.

Ted was a man of cool nerves and great confidence. On one occasion he was Head Guard on a works outing excursion from High Wycombe to Portsmouth Harbour with Jack as his assistant. At Portsmouth they put the coaches away until the evening and had the rest of the day to themselves. Ted was all for going over to the Isle of Wight. 'Do you think we ought to?' asked Jack, whom Ted had always regarded as 'a bit of worrier'.

'Yes, why not? We'll get the ferry back in plenty of time. Come on.'

They got back to Ryde for the ferry — but the ferry had some problem and was late sailing; they would be lucky to catch their train. On tenterhooks, the two men leaped for the quayside at Portsmouth even before the boat was tied up. They ran up the slope to the Harbour station but too late, their train had gone forward with a couple of Southern shunters in charge. The Controller thought that they might catch up with it at Basingstoke where it would be held for a while. On the way up to Basingstoke the two men went ruefully over the likely consequences of their bad luck, including dismissal, and gloomy indeed was the journey. They boarded their train at Basingstoke and worked it back to High Wycombe before taking the empty coaches back to Old Oak Common and the tram ride home.

Amazingly, nothing was said the next day, and after a few days both men relaxed and forgot about the affair. The same furniture factory ordered its train next year and Ted found himself booked to it. Beside his name on the roster sheet was 'SEE ME FIRST' in red letters. Last year's episode came flooding back and he went into the Guv'nor's office in some trepidation. 'I thought I ought to let you have it again — see if you can manage to work the bloody thing all the way back this time. That's all.'

Another Ted, Ted Newell, was a guard on steam railcars shedded at Southall. He never forgot the very first time he went down the Henley branch on his own, rather than as a learner. His train arrived under the Brunelian roof and as there was a bit of time before the next trip he went out into the town. Henley station front is mostly shops with a small entrance to the station at one end. Ted walked away briskly, spent 20 minutes looking at the river, then turned for home, so to speak. He retraced his steps as far as what he thought was the railway station but when he got there all he could see was shops. He looked and looked but he couldn't see the station and, wondering if he was lost, asked a passer-by where the station was. He was in GWR uniform, with 'Guard' on his cap and collar. The passer-by looked at him 'very old-fashioned' and pointed to the far end of the row of shops on the opposite side of the road. 'In there,' he said briefly, and hurried away. 'I felt a proper fool,' said Ted.

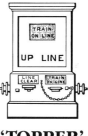

'TOPPER'

Railwaymen were, almost to a man and woman, stalwart spirits, honest and hard-working as the day was long, but there were a few who were not over-bright. In the 1930s there was one such man employed as porter at Haddenham, north of Princes Risborough on the GWR's 'New Line' to Birmingham. He was known to everyone as 'Topper'.

Well, one day four well-to-do locals decided to take a salmon-fishing holiday in Aviemore. They advised the Station Master that they would be travelling by train and taking their car with them, so a 'MOGO' was ordered from Wagon Control and shunted into the dock for loading the day before. 'Topper' got the car inside the 'MOGO' and made it all secure and next day it was coupled to the back of the local train on which the four friends were travelling as far as Banbury where they were to change to an express. I do not know the arrangements for the 'MOGO'.

On arrival at Aviemore they went to their hotel and next day they got a message from the station to say their car had arrived. They went to the station where they were met by a very apologetic Station Master.

They did not at first recognise the car. The radiator and headlamps were smashed, the front wheels were splayed out at an indecent angle and the bumpers were torn, bent and buckled. They got the damage repaired and went on to have a good holiday, catching salmon which they packed in ice and sent south, by train, to Haddenham. 'Topper' was delighted to see the long, narrow wooden boxes dripping with icy water. His friends were having a successful trip.

When they arrived back at Haddenham and stepped out of the little 'dasher', the one-coach 'auto-train' into which they had changed from the express at Banbury, 'Topper' was collecting tickets and greeted them with great enthusiasm, complimenting them on their catch which he had sent . . . The four men looked at him grimly and cut him short.

'How do you secure cars in your vans, "Topper"?' they asked in unison.

The porter was taken aback by their looks. 'Well, I put a good strong rope from the front bumpers and back bumpers to the walls of the van and another from those rods under the front. Then I nail a chog behind the front wheels and the back wheels and put a rope all around the car to the back wall of the van so as to pull it back hard on the chogs.'

The four friends nodded knowingly.

'Yes, that would account for the total demolition of our car. Your Station Master will be getting the bill.'

And off they went for a salmon tea.

KINDRED SPIRITS

In 1984 I noticed a signal at Sleaford that was in particular need of immortality and wrote to York to ask British Rail for permission to enter the lineside to photograph it. In return I received a very rude reply threatening me with <u>imprisonment for criminal trespass</u> (underlined in red) if I entered railway property! The letter also stated that no one was permitted to photograph any part of British Rail property under any circumstances. If British Rail York ever wants a photograph of the somersault signal in Sleaford Yard, I can provide a print — gratis.

The ironic fact is that had I and many others *not* photographed such 'property', hardly any record would have been made of important features of British railways and of our national life. I was once asked by a publisher working for British Rail to provide photographs of certain Western Region locations for a book on railway architecture — *British Railway Heritage* I think it was called. British Rail was convinced it did not have the necessary photographs in its own archive, although I doubted that. Anyhow, I produced 11 photographs which were gratefully received and published — and every one of them was taken whilst I was 'trespassing'!

The railwaymen and women, their wondrous equipment and the whole atmosphere of the railway attracted admiration from many affectionate followers, some of whom were actually able to go and work on the job. The attraction to the railway usually began very early in the life of an individual; it was a matter of early impressions, but those impressions had to fall on a receptive mind and there is the mystery: why some minds are highly susceptible to the steam railway magic whilst others remain impervious to it. It will remain a mystery.

A group of village children, for example, might have grown up near a level crossing which they made their playground and which remained deeply embedded in their affections for ever, and some of them would even become railway workers. Schoolboy railway enthusiasts, eager visitors to some signal box, would grow up and become Bishops or even Cabinet Ministers, but they would never lose their affection for that old signal box and its hospitable signalman. Years later they would recall with affection the coal fire, the mug of tea and the gleaming shine of the equipment. I have had a doctor, an airline pilot, a virtuoso organist, a school teacher, the manager of a factory, several clergymen and a market gardener as 'trespassers' in my various signal boxes.

On duty one Sunday in Challow box, I took a walk 'around the estate' during a quiet period, inspecting the signals and points. I slipped on a sleeper, sprained my ankle and had to hop on one leg back to the box and crawl up the stairs. There was no way I could work the levers for the considerable evening rush period, so I called in an onlooker who often turned up on a Sunday afternoon to watch the trains. I told him which levers to pull whilst I could hop to the bells and to the train register. Between us we kept the service going until 6 pm when my relief arrived.

THE STATELINESS OF THE DISTRICT INSPECTOR

The steam-age GWR District Inspector, who had responsibility for the proper running of the signal boxes in a certain area, was always a man of enormous experience, an ex-signalman who was very interested in his work, pleased with his responsibilities and who usually understood the motivation of the signal box trespasser. I began trespassing at the age of 7 or 8 and did not meet a District Inspector until I was 12 and had a regular signal box so close to home that I could work in it during normal office hours. Inspector Phil Millsom satisfied himself that I was an intelligent trespasser by asking me some simple questions on the signalling regulations and gave me his blessing merely by not ordering me out of the box. He had come to be the Swindon DI via a portering job at Trowbridge and various signalling jobs in the Newbury and Westbury areas.

All these men had long service in a fairly wide district but not so wide that they were not known to any railwayman within it. They grew up together, a generation, and they knew each other, their good points and their bad ones; they respected each other and were good mates. Inspector Arthur Johnson, who was at Paddington in 1966 and did a lot of work during the bringing in of the multiple aspect signalling schemes of that period, began his career on the GWR — which he always suffixed as 'the best' — at Cookham as a Lad Porter in 1917. This was a crossing station, 3 miles north of Maidenhead on the single track to High Wycombe, which did a good trade in freight, parcels and passengers. The signal box was of course a magnet with its ringing bells and colourful equipment, the signalman was very friendly and was willing to teach the boy the system, the rules and regulations, so of course young Johnson was determined to become a signalman.

When he became an adult, in 1918, he moved to West Drayton, a busy main line station with the additional traffic of a branch line to Staines and another to Uxbridge. After two years he got his first taste of signalling as a signal-porter at Reading. His signalling duties entailed working a ground frame to bolt signals at Reading Main Line East and West boxes. There were no track circuits in the main lines, relief lines or platform lines at Reading, the signal boxes were relatively far away from the platforms, their signalmen were very busy, and there were a great many trains. In the absence of track circuits it was possible for a harrassed signalman to lower his signal for a second train to enter an occupied platform. So when a train stopped on any of these lines, the signal-porter's job was to pull the relevant ground frame lever to operate a lock which prevented the lowering of the signal protecting the rear of that train. An identical system was in use at Paddington Arrival Side. Another duty for the signal-porter was to operate a single strike bell between the ground frame — at the east end of the up main platform — and the East Main signal box to convey the shunters' requests for different routes to be set up when passenger coaches, horse-boxes or milk-trucks were being shunted.

After a few months of this, Arthur got a Class 5 signalman's job at Saunderton, a simple 'block post' signal box 5 miles north of High Wycombe and a couple of miles below the summit of the Chilterns, the end of the long, long climb out of Paddington, 31½ miles away. The box was remotely situated near a lonely little halt adjacent to a road bridge, a difficult bike-ride uphill from Wycombe, but at least it was downhill at the end of a shift.

The times were very hard and very unsettled. The national economy was in crisis, railway wages were relatively low, given galloping war-time inflation, and he was fortunate to be on adult wages. Juvenile employees on the Midland Railway on passing into adult status at the age of 18 had been asked to continue to work for boys' wages. The only alternative was to be dismissed. In 1931 all railwaymens' wages were reduced by sixpence (2½p) in the pound and the cut was not restored until 1935. It was something many old timers still remembered with indignation 25 years later but, somehow, the GWR was able to give the impression of being less harsh on its employees, and these same men would also assure me that 'the GWR was the best'.

In spite of a basic wage of about 48 shillings (£2.40) a week, Arthur got married in 1926 and after another two years moved on up the grades, Class 4, 3, 2, 1 and Special Class. This was Hayes & Harlington, an important place with up and down main and relief lines serving four platforms plus a bay platform on the Up Relief line side, goods lines, the GWR's creosoting works and Nestle's factory sidings on the down side, connections to carriage sidings and factories and a busy shunting yard on the up side. The traffic which clamoured to pass through here at high speed, the trundling freight and the stopping pick-up goods, made this the sort of place where the signalmen took his breakfast home with him, uneaten. His wages here, on a good week — night shift, for instance, or where he worked a Sunday — were £5 6s (£5.30), a reasonable wage in 1937. He worked hard for his money and he always felt proud of his efforts in such a busy box. 'I was living in luxury,' he told me.

Unfortunately the war came and a life of 'luxury' gave way to rationing and bombing. On many, many nights, the box trembled and shook as the bombs exploded. Sometimes they fell so close as to bring showers of ballast down on the roof. Arthur worked throughout this, keeping his nerve, running the trains — and with his windows completely blacked out except for one pane so that he could see trains' tail lamps. After the war he became a Special Class Reliefman at Slough covering any box at all from Hayes to Waltham Sidings, west of Maidenhead. From there he became Assistant District Inspector in about 1955 and finally District Inspector, Paddington.

What was there left for the man to learn? Was there any situation on the railway that could 'flap' him after the explosive years of the war and all his other experiences? He was mature, experienced in life as well as railways, unflappable, a gentleman. Well liked and respected by his mates and by the Management. Happy days, and probably gone for ever.

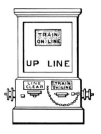

MEMORIES OF TITLEY AND LEOMINSTER JUNCTIONS

The steam railway was the greatest and the most entertaining free show on earth. It was the venue for families out for a drive or a cycle ride at weekends, providing a focus to encourage outings and picnics and improving upon the natural delights of the countryside. And there was a rich variety of sights to see — one thinks of Oxford or Bath Green Park or Leominster. Everyone who was fortunate enough to know those times has their

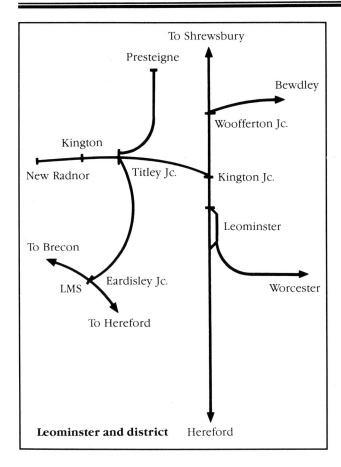

Leominster and district

favourite spot, hallowed from boyhood memories.

My friend John Whiting grew up in the late '20s and '30s near Titley Junction, on the single track branch from Kington Junction (Leominster) to New Radnor. At the east end of Titley station a single track diverged southwards to Eardisley (LMS) while the Presteigne branch ran parallel to the Leominster line, bearing away northwards a mile further east. There were at least 22 trains to be seen at Titley in the course of a normal viewing day in 1928, and courtesy of the Station Master, Mr Diggory, John could watch from the vantage of the signal box and became hooked on the delights of the signalman's job. The station was one where the visitor could bask in the tranquil rural scene, the hot rails creaking in the sun, the red and white of the signals against the green of the fields, and be entertained at convenient intervals by interesting periods of noisy activity.

The first intimations of the forthcoming train were the 'dinging' of the signalling bell, later the louder thud of the signal levers, the porter moving churns or parcels into position, the passengers gathering, then later still the distant whistle of the

engine, heralding the approach of the much-looked-for little locomotive which arrived in a climax of self-importance. The hiss of steam, the singing of the injectors, slamming doors, guard calling to Station Master for 'Right?', his shrilling, thrilling double blast on the pea whistle attached by chain to his jacket, the flute of the engine in reply, the hasty, barking exhaust and the carriages following, wheels ringing over rail joints, then peace returning as the train and the homecoming passengers turned their backs on the little station.

The 'main line' to Kington, westwards, and Pembridge, eastwards, was busy enough to warrant the use of the Electric Train Staff instrument, but the train service on the small branches was infrequent so that a single, wooden train staff was all that was required. All the trains through Titley were delightfully archaic, with green and copper GWR tank engines of the 2-4-0 or 0-4-2 wheel arrangement predominating. Well-known '517' Class 0-4-2 tanks on the branch in 1928-33 included No 533, shedded at Kington for years and withdrawn for scrapping from there in January 1934; No 1424, which spent years in the Much Wenlock and Leominster areas, and which was withdrawn from Leominster shed and scrapped in September 1933; and Nos 3573 and 3574, Worcester engines and the last of their class in the district, withdrawn from Worcester in December 1949. In 1934 some of the new Collett up-dates of the old '517' Class design appeared on the scene, notably Nos 5807, 5808, 5814, 5815 and 5817.

Their load on a Kington branch passenger train was three cream and brown ex-main line eight-wheel clerestory coaches. On the sub-branches the formation was usually a couple of flat-roofed four-wheeled coaches, or perhaps one four-wheeler and one six-wheel clerestory. Their ancient vintage and fairy-tale charm belied the swift acceleration of the '517' Class or 'Metro' tank at the head of the ensemble. Tourists from the big city, sauntering on to the platform, were apt to be left behind in the steamy dash out of the 'sleepy' little station. On the other hand, the friendly, personal contact between railwaymen and their regular passengers could be of the utmost utility.

A regular traveller from Presteign, deep in the Herefordshire lanes, was a solicitor with the unfortunate name of Swindells. For a regular the train crew and station staff would do anything — of

The Eardisley–Titley Junction 'mixed' train at Almeley in 1935. (*Courtesy John Whiting*)

course. One day, Mr Swindells was late for his regular trip to the Police Court in Leominster. The train waited and waited, the Station Master stood by with the necessary ticket, but no Mr Swindells. In the end the train had to go on. It had just cleared the platform when Mr Swindells came spanking into the station forecourt in his gig. The train was stopped by a timely replacement of the signals and was reversed to the platform. The solicitor boarded the train which set off briskly once more, but just as it cleared the platform his secretary came rushing into the station — Mr Swindells had forgotten his gloves! Horrors! The very idea — a solicitor attending court without gloves! Back went the signal, back came the train, in went the gloves and finally the train got away for Leominster.

The Kington branch joined the double track GWR/LMS Joint line at Kington Junction, 34 chains, or 748 yards, north of Leominster station. 'Lemster', 12½ miles north of Hereford and 38½ miles south of Shrewsbury, was a train-watcher's paradise in steam days. It provided the market town with a service of 'all-stations' passenger trains between Hereford and Shrewsbury with connections between these and trains to Worcester/ Birmingham via Bromyard and via Woofferton Junction,

Tenbury and Bewdley. There were also services to Kington, New Radnor, Eardisley and Presteigne. Coal, general freight, mail, perishables and newspapers were brought to the station for distribution to the locality, and cattle, sheep and round timber went for export into the wider world.

The station did not enjoy an express passenger service; one 'caught the stopper' to Hereford or Shrewsbury and changed there. Coming home to Leominster one changed out of the express at the aforementioned places and took the stopping train which followed the 'fast' along the line. There were a good many express trains scheduled to pass through the station, especially on summer Saturdays, and these, of course, were very much enjoyed by lads like John Whiting, who used to cycle out to the station from Titley.

The Station signal box was a timber LNWR production, perched on steel legs high above the down platform, and dated from 1901. It contained a frame of GWR levers numbered to 91 and controlled the station layout and the Worcester branch as far as the next signal box, Fencote. Leominster South box controlled access between the up and down yards and main lines and was a squat, brick, hip-roofed affair dating back to the 1870s, if not before, and

The LNWR signal box at Leominster in 1959. (*Author's Collection*)

John Whiting's view from the Bromyard Road bridge, Leominster South, looking towards the station in 1935. (*Courtesy John Whiting*)

was packed with a 20-lever frame in a floorspace 15 feet square.

The Bromyard main road crossed seven tracks on a bridge at the south end of the station and provided a grandstand view of the great free show. Just below the road embankment on the south side was the South box from whence came the music of signalling bells and the deep thump of levers being pulled. There was a long view southwards towards Hereford and a good, wide view of trains — especially up express trains as they came pounding up the gradient. Northwards lay the broad expanse of sidings, the goods shed, the station and the Worcestershire hills blue in the distance beyond.

To describe the variety of locomotives and rolling-stock which passed across that sumptuous railway stage would now read like a fairy-tale and, indeed, the constantly changing scene in those far-off days was bewitching and totally captivating. It was an enthusiasts' paradise. Because it was a 'Joint' railway there was a mixture of LMS and GWR motive power and vehicles, the GWR predominating. The 'West to North' expresses were the pride of this line, loading as a matter of course to 12-14 coaches over lengthy gradients. The road south from Shrewsbury was, practically speaking, uphill for 13 miles to Church Stretton summit, much of it at 1 in 100, whilst coming the other way, approximately 28 of the 38 miles from Hereford to Church Stretton were uphill.

In the late '20s, the best expresses were hauled by GWR 'Star' and 'Saint' Class 4-6-0 engines with the occasional 'County' Class 4-4-0 or '43' Class 2-6-0 on less heavy trains; on heavy trains one might see double-heading with '43' 2-6-0s and 'County' Class 4-4-0s together. From 1932 the 'Hall' Class began to supercede the old 4-4-0 and 2-6-0 classes on express workings, but the 'Stars' were the most important express engines on the line right up to the Second World War. An occasional 'Castle' was used from the mid-'30s, Nos 4097 and 4099, both Bristol engines, being regular performers. Most stopping passenger trains between Shrewsbury and Hereford, including those run by the 'Joint' company, were hauled by GWR engines, 'Bulldogs' and '43s'. GWR heavy freight was hauled by '28s', 'ROD' Class 2-8-0s and '43' Class 2-6-0s.

LMS motive power through Leominster in 1928-34 was mainly of LNWR origin, although the old Midland Railway was represented by various 0-6-0 tender engines of the '2F', '3F' and '4F' varieties, usually on pick-up goods from Hereford, where there was a traditional Midland Railway presence. The LNWR 'Prince of Wales' Class 4-6-0s ('Tishies') came through on 'Joint Company' local passenger trains, but though these were contemporaries of the GWR 'Stars' and the 'crack' engines of the old LNWR over Shap, they were rarely, if ever, used for the heavy 'North to West' expresses which were the almost exclusive preserve of the aptly-named 'Star' Class. Some of the 'Tishies' were still in LNWR black with LMS/Midland maroon tenders, while others were in LMS maroon with black tenders. By 1935 these had been superceded by the wonderful Class '5' 4-6-0s. In later years the LMS was represented by its best engines, including even the magnificent 'Duchess' Class.

LNWR freight engines outlasted their express passenger brethren. The little 0-6-0 and 0-6-2 Webb tank engines were used on pick-up freights and light work, while the massive Webb/Bowen-Cooke 'Super D' 0-8-0 tender engines and the Beames 0-8-4 tank classes were used for the LMS coal traffic from South Wales.

The wagons behind the engines were always a motley collection of shapes and sizes; many of them were 'private owners' and were painted in 3-foot high letters: CAMROUX, AMALGAMATED ANTHRACITE, BEDWAS COKE, GRAIGOLA, MERTHYR, CANNOP, LITTLETON COLLIERY, LLAY MAIN, CLEE HILL GRANITE CO, and DHU STONE CO. From the Kington branch came OLD RADNOR TRADING CO, and RADNORSHIRE COAL COKE & LIME CO. Last but not least came Leominster's own coal merchant, his coal trucks emblazoned RALPH PREECE DAVIES.

The yards at Leominster would be relatively empty or crowded depending on the time of day. Main line trains stopped at night and early in the morning to pick up and put off traffic, and of course there were many trucks coming off the branches for the main lines. On cattle fair days in Leominster or Kington — or for the annual sheep fair at the latter — the place would be full of 'MEXs', cattle trucks, to be worked down the branch as 'Specials as required'.

Above the bellowing and the bleating came the harsh cough of the GWR shunting engine. No observer from the bridge over the south end of the station complex could fail to notice the complete supremacy of GWR locomotives and wagons over their ex-LNWR contemporaries. The pannier tank was brisk and businesslike in its starts and stops compared to the crude lumberings of an LNWR 0-6-0 tank calling on a pick-up goods. It was a matter of fact, of observation, not bigotry.

A good time of day to arrive on the bridge was 3 pm. There was an LMS goods at work in the up yard and at 3.5 pm the 1.10 pm Crewe–Plymouth express came sweeping down and round the long curve at 60-65 mph behind a 'Saint' or a 'Star'. Shortly after that one would hear the distant, plaintive whistle of the 'First Kington Goods' approaching Kington Junction on the far side of the town. Five minutes after hearing the whistle, the steam and then the train would be seen coming through the station. As it arrived, so the LMS goods pulled northwards out of the sidings.

The engine on the Kington was almost always a pannier tank although occasionally a 'Dean Goods' was used. The load would consist typically of 2-3 loaded 'MEXs', miscellaneous loaded and empty railway-owned wagons, empty 'private owner' coal trucks, their names writ large on the wagon sides, a 'Macaw B' or two loaded with tree-trunks, and, with its steeply pitched roof, a wagon of lime from the Dolyhir quarry. The train would come to a clanking stand in the head-shunt, south of the bridge, prior to the breaking up of the train and the marshalling of the wagons into sidings on both sides of the main lines, according to their destinations.

Five minutes after the branch goods began shunting, the whistle of the New Radnor passenger train would be heard across the town and at 3.28 it could just be seen, drawing to a stand at the station 700 yards away. As it did so the signals cleared into the station from the Worcester/Bromyard branch followed five minutes later by the signals on the down main line. Ten minutes after that the Worcester–Leominster–Kington train came galloping up the branch, under the bridge, enveloping the youthful observers in a cloud of steam and leaving behind the never-to-be-forgotten and much-loved smell of warm oil and soot. The Shrewsbury–Hereford stopping train arrived about 3 minutes later and soon came barking past, the outside-framed 'Bulldog' Class 4-4-0 accelerating Swindon-smartly down the slight grade, under the bridge and away for Hereford, its brisk exhaust dying into

the peaceful fields, leaving only the First Kington Goods to shunt with musical 'chuffs' and jangling couplings in the sidings.

So it was in 1928, 1938 and, yes, even 1948, and so it would be for ever and ever — or so we all thought.

LANGLEY, CHIPPENHAM, CALNE, AND HARRIS'S SAUSAGES

Ray Thomas was 14 in 1947 when he first went into a signal box, Langley Crossing, a mile east of Chippenham station in Wiltshire. The summer of '47 was scorching hot and he and his friends used to go swimming in the Avon, cycling out from the town and crossing the line at the gated level crossing. The location was very pretty, the little signal box, the big, white gates each with their red target, and the elm trees along the line. The boys would often defer swimming for an hour or so to watch the trains — and the down 'Bristolian' would be well worth waiting for as it would be travelling in the 90s there.

The bells 'tinged', the levers thumped, half-heard telephone conversations drifted out of the open windows into the hot, summery day, and Ray Thomas was more than a little intrigued. Observing the boy's interest, the signalman, Tommy Neate, invited him inside to see how the job worked. If the outside had been pretty, the inside of the box was magic and Ray was hooked.

Langley Crossing had no electric lighting, no running water and no lavatory. Lighting was by a pressurised paraffin Tilley lamp (you pumped it up with a bicycle pump) on the wall over the booking desk, water was brought in cone-shaped two-gallon cans from a spring just down the lane, and the 'loo' was an 'Elsan', or sophisticated bucket, in a hut at the bottom of the outside stairs up to the box door. Below the operating floor of the box was the 'locking room' where the mechanical interlocking between the levers could be dimly seen and

Langley Crossing signal box from the up side of the line, looking east. It was an 1880 vintage, brick to floor, standard GWR box, rebuilt by replacing the lower timber panels with brick. (*Courtesy Brian Jackson*)

where the ancient Le Clanche cells (batteries) were housed to power the electrical signalling circuits, and the lamp and signal arm repeaters. The Signal & Telegraph Department lineman collected rainwater in a barrel fed from the signal box gutters to replenish the water in his 'cells'.

Across the lane was a brick hut which had been the crossing keeper's shelter in Broad Gauge days but was, in 1947, the oil store. Next to that again was the platelayers' hut, made of tarred up-ended sleepers with, standing outside, an ancient, hand-turned grindstone on its trestle by which means the permanent way gang sharpened their sickles or 'rip-hooks' when they were 'on grass cutting'. This provision removed the need for them to sharpen up on the tombstone effigies in Langley church. All these men, the p-way gang, the S&T lineman and his mate, were additions to the cast of splendid characters in the theatre of the railway.

Langley Crossing was a good place to learn the rudiments of signalling since it was not too busy — only 30 trains were scheduled to pass the box between 6 am and 2 pm on a weekday in 1954, the same number as in 1936, although there would often be a handful of extras, perhaps a 'runs when required' freight and two or three passenger

excursions, perhaps 35 trains in total or approximately four trains an hour on average. There would be periods of pleasantly busy activity followed by lulls when the signalman could eat his lunch or lean on the window bar and enjoy the countryside or a chat with some passer-by.

It must be said that there were disciplinarian souls who would not allow any authorised person into their signal box. Back in the 1920s there was a signalman at Midgham, John Briggs, whose wife brought him his dinner on a tray covered with a cloth when he was on a 12-hour turn. She had to hand the tray over the threshold — John let absolutely no one into his box!

On the up line at Langley, the section was 5 miles long to Dauntsey, a '12 minute block' for an 'F' or 'H' headcode goods train which formed the vast majority of freight workings on that stretch of line. Beyond Dauntsey was Wootton Bassett incline — 'Dauntsey Bank' to all but the man who wrote the service timetable — 1½ miles of 1 in 100. Because the GWR's Bristol–Bath–London main line was so lacking in steep gradients, unlike almost any other main route in Britain, the local signalmen thought of Dauntsey Bank as a great obstacle — like Shap! This supposition — which was shared by signalmen at least as far east as Challow — was strengthened by the fact that, in 1947, some trains were given the assistance of a banking engine in climbing it.

This little incline assumed a significance out of all proportion to its size and I recall mentioning it, with bated breath, to a Scottish fireman who had been forced south by redundancy. He laughed. 'We don't bother about banks till they are down to two figures', and I thought he was just boasting until I went to Scotland and saw for myself. Travel broadens the mind.

Anyhow, Dauntsey Bank undoubtedly slowed down the progress of eastbound trains so that an up goods train would frequently have to be 'put inside' at Langley or Dauntsey refuge siding to give precedence up the bank to a following 'fast'. Langley Crossing was surprisingly important as a place where goods trains could be side-tracked — especially so on the up road — because Chippenham station had no refuge siding for up trains and only a 44-wagon refuge for down trains. Thus an 'F' or 'H' freight train turned out of the up goods loop at Thingley Junction would run through to Langley — a journey of 3½ miles — in 10 minutes from start to pass, with another 10 minutes to pass Dauntsey, 5 miles further on, making 20 minutes in all. That was if the driver was in a good mood. Loose-coupled trains could run quite remarkably slowly at times and the official 'point to point' times for freight trains printed in the GWR and BR Western Region working timetables were exceedingly optimistic.

If an up express was leaving Bath when the goods pulled out of Thingley loop, that express would be racing past Thingley Junction as the goods trudged past Langley Crossing at 25 mph with another 11 minutes before it cleared Dauntsey, by which time the express would have carried out its Chippenham call and would have been 'waiting the road' at Langley Crossing's up starting signal. Under such circumstances the Dauntsey signalman would 'put the freight away' and, of course, the process of stopping and reversing it would mean that the time taken for the train to clear the section between Langley and Dauntsey would be even longer. So, if the 'fast' was leaving Bath when the 'F' headcode left Thingley loop, it would be 'put away' at Langley.

It is worth noting that this example shows how the signalman at Thingley had to make his decisions on traffic regulation. It was useless for him to 'turn one out of the up loop for Langley' if that train was too long for Langley's refuge, unless he knew that the down line traffic would allow the Langley signalman to cross that goods train to the down main to await the passing of the up express. Such was the skill and 'road knowledge' demanded of an ordinary signalman in the days of steam and, needless to say, with the best will in the world, their arrangements and calculations came unstuck occasionally. These were the considerations which passed through the signalman's mind when he was signalling an up goods train. His job was made more difficult by the inadequacy of train accommodation. The down refuge held a modest 58 wagons, engine and van, but the up refuge held only 43, which was very poor, given the average length of freight trains. So when an up goods was too long for the siding it had to be reversed through

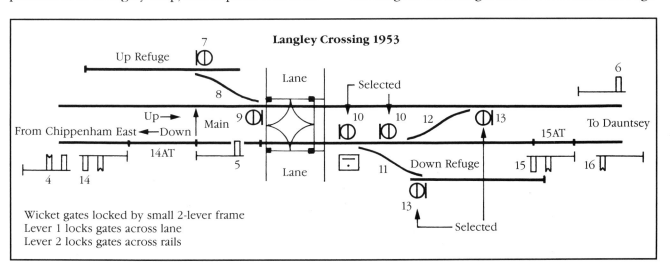

Langley Crossing 1953

Up Refuge

From Chippenham East ← Down   Up →   Main

Lane   Selected   To Dauntsey

Down Refuge

Selected

Wicket gates locked by small 2-lever frame
Lever 1 locks gates across lane
Lever 2 locks gates across rails

the crossover to the down main line — if traffic on that line permitted.

The regulations stated that a signalman must not give 'Line Clear' to the box in the rear unless the line at his signal box was clear for 440 yards ahead of the home signal and all points within that distance were set for the safety of the approaching train. When the down line at Langley Crossing was thus occupied by a shunted train, it extended into the 440-yard safety zone of the down home signal (No 15) and was then said to be 'fouling the clearing point'.

The Langley Crossing signalman then dropped the 'Clearing Point Fouled' flap over the white 'Line Clear' sending key on the signalling instrument, which prevented the key being used to communicate with Dauntsey. In 1953 the down home signal was re-positioned several hundred yards further east to ensure that when an up train was standing on the down main there was the regulation minimum of at least 440 yards between it and the home signal. Thus 'Line Clear' could be sent to Dauntsey when the down line was occupied at Langley. At the same time, electric 'track circuits' — 15AT and 14AT — were provided in the down main line. When these circuits were occupied by a train, electric locks prevented the down line signals from being pulled, but a careful 'belt and braces' signalman also placed a lever collar on his down distant and down home signal levers to remind him not to pull them.

At the same time as these alterations were made, lever 3, which locked both wicket gates against pedestrians, was removed and replaced by a separate frame of two short levers, one for each gate. The increase of one lever and the presence of two brass-cased track circuit repeaters was a source of great worry to Tommy Neate who promptly applied to have the signal box re-classified from Class 4 to Class 3. He obtained the up-grading, with some help from the local community who made extra use of the crossing on the appointed day, thus giving him more work than usual.

Ray Thomas was never allowed to make train running decisions. His first lesson was in how to 'pull off' — and that was not merely a matter of pulling the levers. There was a 'knack' to be learned, especially when swinging over the distant signal levers, each with 1,000 or 1,500 yards of strong wire attached. Then he learned the routine

of bell codes and what they meant, and by that time he was a regular visitor and was beginning to learn the service, the sequence of trains. Having shown his willingness to learn, he was given the books of rules and regulations and told to learn them, which he did, taking lessons and explanations from the signalman between trains. Such was the enthusiasm — not only of Ray Thomas — but also of Tommy Neate.

I can vouch for the fact that in those days, when the job seemed eternal and unchanging, the men's conversations were frequently taken up with discussions of the regulations as a form of entertainment. We were all keen to do a good job, although none of us thought of ourselves as 'railway enthusiasts'; indeed, the phrase was unknown amongst us. We were all committed to the railway and doing our best for it. Those seriously interested visitors we allowed into the boxes were simply 'good old boys' — in the Berkshire/Wiltshire idiom which made no reference to age but only to character. However, to temper this glorious picture of devotion to the job, it must be admitted that Signalman Neate had some ulterior motive for his efforts on Ray Thomas's behalf.

By the September of 1947, Tommy had Ray fully trained and let him work the box whilst he chatted on the 'bus-line 'phone or got on with work in his lineside vegetable garden within ear-shot of the bells. Ray soon got to know other signalmen and gave up all his spare time, after due attention to school work, to signal box visiting, cycling miles to work boxes as far apart as Thingley Junction, Little Somerford, Wootton Bassett West and Melksham, Devizes, Woodborough, Seend, Calne and Lavington, as well as the Chippenham boxes. Every one of these places, large or small, was kept immaculately clean and highly polished; to have done otherwise would have been the height of caddishness, like smoking a cigarette on the footplate of an engine in the old days. Pipe smoking was in order, of course.

The great delight of signal box visiting was in seeing the perfection of the polished and very colourful equipment, in witnessing the variations of the working and equipment from box to box, and in the delightful characters that one met. There was a great pleasure in working the splendid equipment to control the passing of the magnificent trains, and there was also the pleasure of

The interior of Langley Crossing box with signalman Fred Crockett in about 1947. (*Courtesy Ray Thomas*)

hearing the superb fund of stories which were constantly being related over the 'bus line telephone, or over a mug of tea between the signalman and his visitor. If the right man was on duty, a visit to him and his box was as good or better than a visit to the theatre.

My late and much lamented friend, Ivo Peters, would agree whole-heartedly with this. He had a lineside walking permit but that did not cover signal box interiors which he nevertheless visited and felt very grateful for the friendships he made with such great characters as Percy Savage, Harry Wiltshire and Charles Eyre at Midford in the 1940s and '50s, and Mervyn Holbrook at Bradford Junction in the 1970s, to mention but a few — all the 'S&D' men were his friends.

Both Midford and Bradford Junction signal boxes were legendary throughout the area for their state of polish, but Bradford Junction was perhaps the more striking because it was very much larger, controlling a triangular junction. The floor was so glass-gleaming clean that no footplateman was permitted to bring his dirty boots across the

threshold, and the stove was so well polished with 'Zebo' that it gleamed blackberry black. Rather than spoil the shine, the signalmen never lit it and on cold days preferred to shiver over a 'Valor' oil stove instead; or so it was alleged in 1947-54. By 1974 the fanaticism had gone, but Mervyn still gained full marks from Ivo for the highly polished state of his signal box.

Having said all that, one ought to balance it by saying that the shift system meant six days at 10 pm-6 am, Sunday 6 am-6 pm, followed by six days of 2 pm-10 pm, Sunday 6 am-6 pm, followed by six days 6 am-2 pm, before having Saturday afternoon and Sunday off duty — if you were not brought back for a Sunday engineering job. This made 20 days continuous work where even going to sleep at home was part of the job, getting ready for the next shift, and there were times when even I felt that I was on something resembling a treadmill. Night shift was often the most difficult, especially in the latter half of the week when the desire for sleep, just a few minutes around 3 or 4 am, would become overwhelming and therefore essential.

Good lighting and ventilation played a large part in keeping the signalman awake at night. At my old box at Uffington, as at Langley Crossing, we worked by the light of a Tilley lamp so I can compare that with the electric lighting which was much better. With a single Tilley lamp, the pale, yellow light was in itself enough to send one to sleep, but there was also the soporific hissing it made and the heat it gave off, while the smell of warm paraffin was overpowering in a small space. One would go to the door of the box, breath some fresh night air and look up at the stars — if there were any — and listen to the night noises, then a signalling bell would ring and one would go inside and mistakenly reply on the wrong bell — much to the annoyance of your mate who was woken from his small hours nap 10 minutes earlier than need be.

Chippenham seems to have had its fair share of signal box trespassers, which term has to include the sons of signalmen. One day, John Sadler, a Westinghouse Brake & Signal Company employee, was working Thingley Junction while the signalman looked on. A passenger train from Westbury was approaching and Sadler was leaning on the bar at the window, ready to examine the coaches for 'signals of alarm', when to his astonishment he saw his boss, Kenneth Leech, CME at Westinghouse, driving the engine!

Kenneth had a lineside walking permit and devoted his efforts almost entirely to recording the locomotives and their crews, but even he photographed signal box interiors and the signalmen on occasions, probably as a token of his appreciation for the hospitality and train running information he received from them. He was a frequent visitor to Langley Crossing, Chippenham East and West and Bath Station boxes. He always supplied his railway-man friends with 10 × 8 prints of themselves and their engine/signal box and dozens of his prints must be lying around all over Western Region territory, hopefully well treasured.

But Kenneth was a locomotive man rather than an admirer of signal boxes. A signal box connoisseur would balance the interest of working a particular box against the delightfulness of the personality who was in charge at that time. Jack Gale, an elderly relief signalman, was a particularly good raconteur and could keep a visitor spellbound with his tales of the boxes he had operated in his 40-odd years, the traffic he handled, the systems, and the funny or tragic events. Like all railwaymen of his generation he spoke with affection about the skill required to work 'the single needle', and regretted his loss in having only the mundane telephone to operate. When he was speaking on the 'phone, his fingers seemed to be tapping out the Morse code as if he was 'on the needle'.

Nationalisation of the railway had no immediate effect on the men's morale. They were still all Great Western men hoping that public funds would be injected into the network to restore it to its pre-war condition after the savage wear and tear of six years of war and comparative neglect. They also hoped they would receive higher wages and better conditions. Most men had a sentimental attachment to the old name — 'GWR' — and were sad at its passing, but they lived in hope of better times ahead after years of war and the hard times of the 1930s. And they took their wonderful dual spirit of devotion to duty and cheerfulness with them into the new age. As midnight on 31 December 1947 approached, the station staff at Chippenham laid hundreds of detonators on one rail from the East to the West box, a distance of 570 yards, and on the stroke of 12 they sent the station pilot engine over them. Ray Thomas was in Langley Crossing box at that unique midnight hour and heard clearly the crackling bangs going off over a mile away.

Nationalisation, Great Western men believed, meant that GWR practices would be extended throughout the United Kingdom, and it was a matter of some disgust for them to see that LMS practices were preferred. Upon Nationalisation, ex-Southern or 'Midland' men were entitled to move into GWR signal boxes or stations in the course of promotion. These men were welcomed hospitably as if they were refugees from some awful disaster — which is what, after all, the ''ell of a mess' LMS was — and they were frequently reminded of their good fortune in being now part of a 'proper' railway.

In this regard I am reminded of the famous GWR story dating from Broad Gauge days, still current amongst Western men 60 years later. A meeting of various railway company officers was held at Paddington to which were invited some representatives of those rather unmentionable railways south of the Thames. The Very Senior Great Western Officer in the chair had introduced to him the representative of the London, Brighton

& South Coast Railway. The Very Senior GWR person removed his monocle, gave his guest a very superior GWR smile, and said: 'How very *interesting* to meet a *tramwayman*!'

With Nationalisation came alterations to the GWR signalling regulations — including new bell codes. Everything new was suspected of emanating from the LMS and was therefore unsafe. The 'Train Divided' regulations were radically changed — for the worse — by permitting a train to pass signals at 'Danger'. GWR old hands were horrified. 'Bloody Midland!' The GWR code for a parcels train — 5 bells — was superceded by 1-3-1. Only the LMS could have thought of anything as silly as 'dum-diddy-dum-dum' as a bell code.

In the early days of the introduction of this code, Western men did not 'acknowledge by repetition' the 1-3-1 code, but gave a sarcastic 1-1! Anything which was not Great Western was *no good*. Needless to say, the men of the erstwhile Somerset & Dorset Joint Railway and of the M&GN were equally convinced that there was no railway as good as theirs. No army regiment had a higher morale.

Life at Langley Crossing was as near perfect as anything could be in this wicked world, a rural idyll such as one might expect from the remoter reaches of the M&GN or the Midland & South Western Junction Railway of sacred memory, but yet with the added attraction of being on one of the great main lines of England, signalling all kinds of trains from humble freights hauled by 'big old 28s' to the 'hard-hitting' 'Castle' and 'King' Class engines on the 'down Londons' racing past at 80 or even 90 mph, the impetus of Dauntsey Bank behind them. From the summer of 1954, the down 'Bristolian', 8.45 am from Paddington, the fastest train in Britain, at first 'King' and then 'Castle'-hauled, passed by at 10.3 am, going like the wind.

To keep a proper balance it is worth mentioning that there were the rare occasions on which the 'Bristolian' engine failed *en route*, and when even more remarkable running was done by totally unprepared and 'unsuitable' engines, or other occasions when the booked engine lost time owing to a shortage of breath in the iron steed. The signalman watched and listened to the working of this most illustrious of trains with great interest, and any departure from the usual high standards, and sometimes even a change of driving technique —

heard in the sound of the exhaust — was noted and commented on.

When the dust had settled behind such trains, bucolic peace returned to the Langley lane. The signalman — or his unofficial assistant — unlocked the gates by pulling the blue (locking) lever 1 and then 'swung the gates', heaving on the handles of the big, iron wheel. The wheel had a heavy boss which doubled as a cog driving against an iron rack which was thus raised or lowered to close or open the gates across the lane. Now the rack sank downwards to drive the rodding and swing the heavy gates off the lane and across the rails. The safety ratchet clanked ringingly until the gates crashed against their stop in 'the six-foot'. Blue locking-lever No 2 was then reversed to lock the gates across the rails to allow, perhaps, a horseman and a car to cross the line.

The lane led to two farms, a few farm cottages and a footpath to the river Avon, so it was a favourite place to walk a dog, ride a horse, stroll with your girlfriend or take as a route to some good fishing — and this besides the use made of it by those who actually lived at the farms. The gate wheel was, of course, at the road end of the box and, having opened the gates, the signalman went to the door to exchange at least a wave and probably some banter with whoever was passing. He was well known to all who passed and he knew — or thought he knew — a great deal about them.

Gossip at any level crossing signal box was part of the job and even more so here, where only a dozen or so 'regulars' used the crossing and their comings and goings at any time of the day or night could be noted. Discreet questions could be asked and scandalous explanations given for seemingly mysterious movements. Like the driver of a tractor who regularly used to leave his machine in the field, hidden but with its engine running, for maybe an hour. Supposed explanation of mystery: he was off down the river with his girlfriend and left his engine running so his wife would think he was working.

At almost any time or season, the box was a superb place to work. On a summer evening, long shadows fell across the scene from the tall, lineside elms, while the slight smell of warm creosote from the sleepers drifted through the air as the hot rails creaked. Children would be playing in the field across the lane, their otherwise shrill cries somehow muted in the warm air to become almost as pleasant as bird song.

In spite of enjoying such distractions, the signalman did actually attend conscientiously to his work. Take, for instance, the signalling of the loose-coupled, unbraked, 'H' headcode Banbury–Westbury coal. The official 'margin' was that if the following 'fast' was less than 25 minutes behind the goods when the latter passed Dauntsey, then the goods had to be stopped and reversed into the down refuge. If the following express was the 'Bristolian', this meant that if it was passing Wantage Road, milepost 60½, as the down Banbury passed Dauntsey, milepost 87¾, the goods had to be refuged at Langley, milepost 92¾. If it was too long it would be crossed to the up main.

The Banbury was a loose-coupled train and would take 12 minutes from passing Dauntsey to stopping at Langley with its van clear of the siding points, by which time the 'Bristolian' would be near Swindon. By the time the Langley Crossing signalman had 'shut the Banbury inside' and had sent 'Train out of Section', 2-1 on the bell, to Dauntsey, the Express of Expresses would by flying through Wootton Bassett, 3½ minutes from Dauntsey's distant signal. The signalman at Dauntsey would very promptly 'ask the road', 4 bells, for the 'Bristolian' and, receiving 'Line Clear' from Langley Crossing, would 'pull off', lowering his distant signal about 2¾ minutes before Britain's fastest scheduled train passed it. At Dauntsey's down distant signal the train would have been running at an accelerating 90 mph so the driver did not want to find that signal against him. Through Dauntsey station the 'Bristolian' occasionally ran at 100 mph, and even slightly higher speeds were not unknown.

No one took chances with the holy 'Bristolian' — it was as sacred after Nationalisation as it and the 'Cheltenham Flyer' had been in GWR days. Where other express trains were concerned the signalmen might 'take a chance' to keep a freight running, to 'run it on a tight margin' to the next refuging point or the point where it left the main line. The decision was made from a compound of variable factors some of which I will try to explore.

Trains for the Westbury direction turned off the down main line at Thingley Junction, 3½ miles beyond Langley Crossing and 8 miles beyond Dauntsey. A tight but just feasible margin for an 'F' or 'H' headcode train from passing Dauntsey to clearing on to the Westbury line at the junction would have been 18 minutes ahead of a 'fast', always provided that the latter was booked to stop at Chippenham. For a 'F' or 'H' train starting out of the refuge at Langley Crossing, the bare margin would have been 15 minutes ahead of an express stopping at Chippenham. The freight would want an extra 2 minutes margin ahead of a following express which was not stopping at Chippenham. These margins would be tight enough to qualify the perpetrator for the deprecatory title of 'Purger'!

The expresses' timings varied. The 7.30 am Paddington to Paignton was booked to cover the 16¾ miles from Swindon to Chippenham, start to stop, in 18 minutes. The 9.5 am and 11.15 am Paddingtons were booked 15 minutes pass to pass, and the 7.50 pm Paddington–Bristol was booked 14 minutes pass to stop.

The general rule was that if the express was one that called at Swindon and Chippenham and if it had not yet left Swindon when the Westbury-bound freight passed Dauntsey, then, provided the latter was 'doing well', the Langley Crossing man would probably be prepared to 'give it a run'. If the following fast was non-stop Swindon and Chippenham and was no closer than 'passing Marston West' when the goods came off Dauntsey, again the Langley man would probably 'give the goods a chance'.

The two Chippenham boxes were 572 yards apart and this introduced a double difficulty — the absolute necessity of providing adequate braking distance between the distant ('caution') signal and the home, the first 'stop' signal, of each. To provide this, the 'block section' became, effectively, Langley Crossing to Thingley Junction, for the following reason.

On the down line, the East box outer distant signal was the correct braking distance from its home signal, but the West box distant signal could be placed no further away than below the East box starting signal, a mere 787 yards from its home signal. The correct braking distance was almost twice that. On the up line the West box distant signal was placed 1,100 yards from the up home, but the East box distant was only 590 yards from its home signal. It was a common situation to be found at hundreds of locations all over Britain.

Because of this lack of braking distance, both

East and West box distant signals had to work in unison. In some places, given this situation, the distant signals of the two boxes would have been worked by electric motors and the motors electrically interlinked, but at Chippenham the signals were individually and manually operated, and control was by a signalling routine.

When East box asked West box 'Is Line Clear?' for a down train, West box could not give 'Line Clear' until he had obtained 'Line Clear' from Thingley Junction. If a down train was occupying the section between West box and Thingley when East box 'asked the road' for another down train, West box replied with 2-2-2, 'Line Clear to Clearing Point Only'.

Receiving 2-2-2, the East box man could either accept it or refuse it. If he accepted it, he had to hold all his signals at 'Danger' until the train had passed his distant signal at 'Caution'. His decision on whether to accept or refuse 2-2-2 depended on how far away was the approaching train. If it was so far away that the previous train would have cleared Thingley Junction before the following one reached the East box distant signal, the East box man would refuse it and offer the train again to West box after a few minutes, hoping then to receive the full 'Line Clear' so that he could lower all his signals and give the approaching train a clear run.

If East box did refuse the 2-2-2 code, West box would stand by, alert, and send 'Line Clear' back to East for the next train as soon as the first train cleared Thingley and he had obtained 'Line Clear' from that box. The object and outcome of the routine was that the East box distants were used to cover the West box home on the down line. The same system was used on the up line, with East box using the 2-2-2 code back to West box.

It was a uniquely Great Western system which managed to survive the 'LMS-isation' of everything after Nationalisation and was still in use in 1972. The technique of working the 'three twos' routine required the signalmen to develop what to outsiders seemed like an uncanny knowledge of timing, of where a train would be, of how matters would be progressing not only at the next box but for miles down the line. Such a sense had to be developed if a signalman was to work the job properly in those days of manual signalling. I still have a 'signalman's clock' in my head!

The Langley Crossing signalman's well-trained instincts would thus examine the traffic situation as soon as Dauntsey 'asked the road' for a down goods train. He would look at the clock and examine his mental timetable to see if there was a following 'fast' likely to be delayed by the goods. If there was, he would make inquiries 'up the line' by telephone. When Dauntsey sent 2 beats — 'Train entering Section' — for the down goods train, the Langley Crossing signalman would ask his mate at Dauntsey (who was almost certainly chatting on the 'bus line 'phone and easily accessible) for a final check on the speed of the train. 'How's that down one running, Bob?' He would also call Chippenham East and West boxes to make sure they would 'run' the approaching goods train, and would telephone Swindon West box to find out 'where's that down London now?'

If all the answers were the right ones, the decision would then be irrevocably made to 'pull off'. The inquiries took less time than might be thought, since a call took no more than a press of a button, and in any case the other men were usually already chatting on the 'bus line 'phone. When 'phoning Swindon West, his call was answered immediately by the booking boy whose desk and seat were alongside the telephone. This was the sort of care (or rigmarole) that any Western signalman took over his 'margining' before getting back to what he would jokingly call 'important matters', like the cure for blight on Ronnie Astridge's 'floribunder' roses.

As the goods passed, the Langley Crossing signalman sent the train 'on line' to East box, sent 'Train out of Section' to Dauntsey and stood by to answer bells and work instruments promptly. Two minutes later, if indeed the down 'fast' had pulled out of Swindon as the goods was passing Dauntsey, both the bells in Langley box would ring out more or less together. The Chippenham East bell would ring out 'Ting-ting, ting' — 'Train out of Section' for the goods — at about the same time as the Dauntsey bell rang 1 beat, 'Call Attention'. This would be answered, then the 4 beats 'Is Line Clear for an Express Passenger Train?' would be received and acknowledged and the white key on the old Spagnoletti block instrument would be pressed down and held by the peg. This caused the white 'flag' bearing the legend 'Line Clear' to swing into view in the little window in the front of the instrument.

The Dauntsey signalman had 'asked the road' for the down 'fast' as it had been passing Hay Lane signal box and had sent it 'on line' to Langley Crossing 6-7 minutes later as it ran past his box at around 75-80 mph. Receiving the 2 beats, the Langley Crossing signalman acknowledged, released the white key, pegged down the red key of his block instrument and gave one beat on the tapper of the Chippenham East bell. The white 'flag' in the Langley/Dauntsey instrument swung out of sight to be replaced by a red one bearing the legend 'Train on Line' as the Chippenham East bell 'tinged' out its response. Langley tapped out 4 beats to Chippenham East and, as the reply came back and the Langley/Chippenham East block instrument swung to 'Line Clear', the Langley signalman moved to his gate mechanism. He closed the gates across the lane, locked them and then lowered his down main signals.

The 'V'-ended yellow and black arms of Chippenham East's outer and inner distant signals were placed below the red and white arms of Langley Crossing's home and starting signals respectively, and the former remained firmly at 'Caution' while the red arms swung down to a good, deep angle. Chippenham East could not lower his distant signals until Chippenham West gave him 'Line Clear' and, as we know, Chippenham West could not do this until he had obtained 'Line Clear' from Thingley Junction. This of course could not be obtained until the goods had cleared away on to the branch line at Thingley. The driver of the rapidly approaching express had a very long, clear view of Langley's home signal, with the Chippenham East distant 'on' (at 'Caution') beneath it, and he would blow an indignant blast on the whistle, easily heard in Chippenham, as he came racing down towards the 'Caution' signal — known as 'blowing down the back board'.

Brakes hard on, the engine came over the crossing at 60 mph, whistling again. But during those vital seconds the signalmen ahead were working hard. Thingley had 'knocked out' for the goods and the Chippenham signalmen were working frantically. The West box signalman 'rattled out' the 4 beats to Thingley, the Thingley signalman, who was well aware of the situation back at Langley, was expecting this and responded at once with 'Line Clear' back to West box. West at once gave 'Line Clear' to East and both signalmen

'pulled off' as fast as they could, the East box inner distant 'dropping down the chimney' of the 'Castle' Class engine. It had been very close, but no great delay had been suffered by the express whilst the goods had been saved 30 minutes or more. If asked by Control whether the down London had been checked, the Langley Crossing man would say, 'He had a bit of a tickle, nothing much'. Of course, if the express was one that stopped at Chippenham, no delay would have been caused.

A signalman needed to be physically fit and mentally alert, conscientious and ready to make rapid decisions if he was to work his box properly. It was not necessarily a sign of a lack of conscientiousness to admit young lads — or old ones — into the signal box, but rather a sense of friendliness towards someone who was obviously very interested in one's work. In the larger signal boxes, with a lot of point levers to be pulled for shunting movements as well as the main line work to the attended to, the need was to be quick, walking briskly to and from the bells and levers, so as not to hold up the work of the signalmen with whom one was working nor to delay the shunting at one's own station.

But of course, as the higher grade boxes were manned by the older men, it was inevitable that some of the signalmen were not in the best of health, and worked slowly, causing annoyance to their signalman colleagues who were impatient of delay when they waited overlong for an answer to a bell signal — the bells should be answered immediately and a delay of more than 15 seconds was overlong.

Chippenham up to 1955 was a very busy junction station catering for two market towns. The 5¼-mile-long, single track Calne branch forked south from the London–Bristol main line at Chippenham East box and was one of the most profitable small branch lines on the GWR or Western Region. It handled most of the traffic for C.&T. Harris Ltd, whose factory at Calne produced world-famous meat-pies. The live animals went down the branch by the truck load and the meat pies came up loaded in dedicated four- and eight-wheel wagons, or filling the guard's brake on the branch passenger train. Every Christmas the Calne and Chippenham railwaymen, even the signalmen at Langley Crossing and Thingley Junction, received Christmas presents of pork-pies from

Harris Ltd. The ASLEF strike of 1955, after the NUR had made a pay deal with BR without a strike, forced Harris Ltd to look for alternative transport. They bought lorries and the branch went into a fatal decline. No Christmas hampers — no jobs.

The Calne branch had always been a very profitable branch line and, prior to 1955, Chippenham was busy in a way difficult to believe for anyone who has not seen the old-fashioned railway at work, carrying a large part of the goods of the nation. There were two engines shunting day and night (with rest breaks), one in the up yard and the other in the down yard. Another engine acted as the Local Pilot, making transfer trips from yard to yard, taking freight to Calne and working the 'fly' goods down to Bathampton and back, all stations. Another engine performed passenger shunting and acted as banker for Box incline as required, whilst the engine of a Trowbridge to Chippenham passenger train acted as 'Passenger Pilot' in case of failure of some main line train, shunted the goods yard if required when the actual shunting engine went to shed or the men took their break, and then worked an evening passenger train home to Trowbridge.

There were various trains which started or terminated at Chippenham for or from Weymouth, Westbury or Frome, and there were 13 round trips by passenger train on the Calne Branch, some of which ran 'mixed', that is, hauling freight wagons behind the coaches. Two more trips each way ran purely for freight. So busy was the work for the train crews on the Calne branch, with the shunting of Harris's vans, coal and cattle trucks and the 'running round' of the train by the engine, that on more than one occasion the fireman forgot to hook the engine to the train and went off without it.

Express passenger and mixed traffic locomotives overhauled at Swindon Works would frequently make a 'running in' turn on a stopping train through or terminating at Chippenham; the engine and coaches would be shunted away and the engine would go to turn on the table. Many and splendid were the ex-Works, ex-GWR 'high-stepping' engines that graced the scene at Chippenham, dwarfing the busy little panniers as they snorted up and down the sidings forming trains and transfer trips. Also to be mentioned were the horrifyingly LMS-looking 'Britannia' Class.

The smaller of the two Chippenham boxes was the West box, just off the west end of the down platform, high above the main road, with a good view of the town and almost as high as the nearby church tower. The levers within it were numbered 1-26, but there were 9 spaces leaving 17 working levers. The layout was very simple but yet very curious, and I suspect this was due to some quirk of ancient railway history, for what at first glance appeared to be the usual double track main line between the two platforms was actually the down main and a down-facing bay. The up main line went behind the up platform. Thus an up Westbury to Chippenham passenger train booked to terminate there ran to the rear face of the up platform and had then to be shunted, by roundabout methods, to the down bay for the return journey. To make matters even more complicated, arriving Calne trains had to use the down main platform, but then had to depart from the 'Calne bay' between the down and up main lines.

The Westbury and Calne services required stock to be shunted to their departure bays, vans of pies and milk to be put off the trains and on to main line trains, and engines to 'run round'. To speed the work movements could be made in the 'wrong' direction, ie up the down line or down the up line between the two signal boxes. The 'Warning Arrangement', 3-5-5 on the bell, permitting the approach of a train under severe caution when the line was blocked, was not permitted although it would have been very useful in some instances.

On one shift the signalman was Ted Allen, a slow worker, not a popular man and considered bad tempered by his mates. This feeling arose simply because no one had ever bothered to understand Ted's problems. He was a very decent sort really, but he was not in the best of health — which made him slow — and the discomfort he suffered, coupled with the impatience of his mates, made him bad tempered.

He heard about Ray Thomas, by then a 17-year-old amateur signalman of considerable experience, being conversant with the working at half-a-dozen boxes, and sent a message asking if he, Ray, would come to see him in the West box. Ray went, wondering what the old chap could want, and discovered that he required a competent assistant! 'It's me feet, you see, Ray,' he confided to him in his soft, Wiltshire accent, 'I can't bend 'em, they're like two solid lumps on the end o' me legs.' Ray could

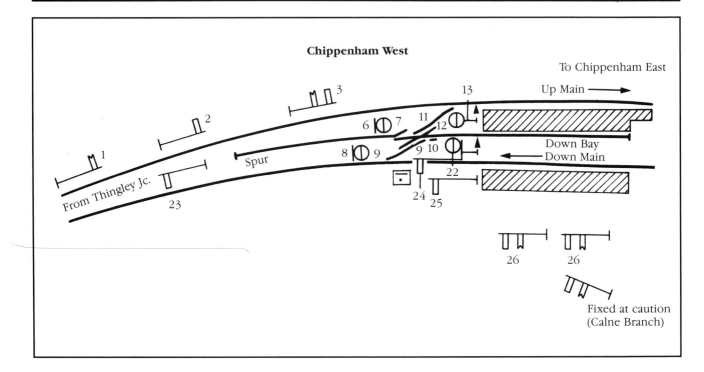

Chippenham West

see how difficult it was for Ted to walk, and even more difficult to pull the levers, since a great deal of strength was required for some of them, and also a swinging back movement which certainly required the feet to be flexible. The same applied when restoring a point or a facing-point bolt lever to the normal position — one really had to force it forward, leaning over on to the balls of the feet.

A signal lever would usually go back all the way simply by the weight of the wire if one released the catch, although there would be much screeching and banging. I cannot imagine how Ted managed if his feet were numb and inflexible — but he did and, of course, he was slow to reach the bells and slow to work the levers. He avoided heavy pulls if he could and never lowered his distant signal for a train which was stopping at the station: 'There's no point in making work — he's stopping here anyhow.'

Ted watched Ray work the bells and pull off, saw that he worked with confidence, and settled himself down in the chair with the telephone, the clock and the train register close to hand. For any special local workings, such as a shunting movement up the down line, Ted knew he could instruct Ray as required and the boy would soon understand what was needed. The arrangement pleased them both and Ray, being of a sympathetic nature, soon had Ted confiding all his troubles to

him and in turn discovered that the old boy had a delightfully dry sense of humour.

When a job came up in East box, poor old Ted with his feet put in for it. Many people, including Ray, were surprised because East box was 'a heavy number'. The frame was numbered 1-63 (including 9 spaces) so there was further to walk and there were far more lever movements to be made — including one set of points (No 46, Goods shed to Down Main) that were 270 yards from the box, making for a very heavy pull. There was also what would be a very difficult duty for Ted, going down 20 steps and across 60 feet of tracks to the down main to meet the incoming Calne train eight times a shift, and again, to the foot of the stairs, to hand up the branch key token to the out-going branch train.

Anyhow, Ted got the job and managed it somehow although he must have found the work enormously trying. For a start he persuaded the branch locomotivemen to bring him the key token, and trained them to stretch up for the outbound key as they passed the box. He also did not have to clean the box and the windows, for this work had always been done by a porter from the station who also went out to Stanley Bridge halt, 2½ miles down the branch, to light the platform lamps. Chippenham East box was thus kept tidy but was not well polished.

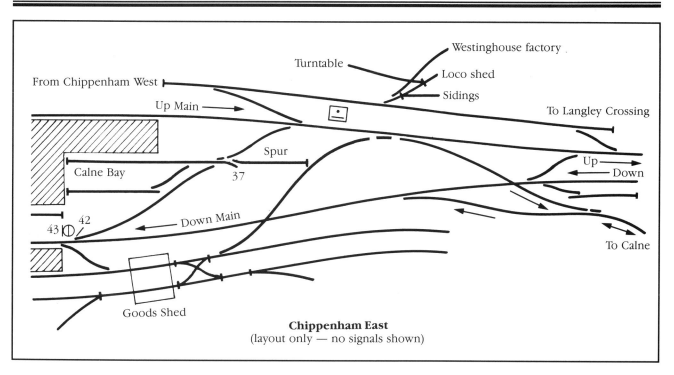

Chippenham East
(layout only — no signals shown)

Ted Allen on the frame at Chippenham East box *circa* 1950. The track diagram is visible top left, and there is a GWR pendulum clock over Ted's head, some key token carriers behind him, a fine wooden armchair, and the booking desk in the foreground. (*Courtesy Ray Thomas*)

The view eastwards from Chippenham East box window, with the Calne branch swinging right behind the line of box vans. (*Courtesy Ray Thomas*)

The East box signalman was kept very busy with more or less continuous shunting, transfer trips, branch and main line trains — and he had the train register to maintain as well, as no booking lad was provided. There was a single-strike bell on the instrument shelf so that the shunters could make their wishes known when shunting at the station end of the layout which was over 200 yards from the box. The code 1-2 meant 'Close Points', and 3-1 meant 'Set Points into Down Siding'. There was another code for 'Set Points to Middle Siding' and another 'Set Points Middle Siding to Calne Bay (Platform 4)'.

The East box layout was pleasantly complicated with shunting yards on both sides of the line, the engine shed and turntable roads, the junction to Calne and the Calne bay between the main lines. As I have already mentioned, a passenger train from Calne ran to the down main platform and had then to shunt to the Calne bay. This was straightforward if the train was formed as a 'push-pull' unit: trap-points 37, points 42 and signal 43 being the first sequence to pull (see the diagram on pages 40-1). When the train was in the Spur, 43 and 42 were restored and lever 38 reversed to signal the train

back into the bay platform.

If the Calne train was 'engine and coaches', the engine had first to run round its train before pushing it into the bay, which more than doubled the work.

With Ted at the East box, the signalmen at Langley Crossing had considerable difficulty in getting the Langley up distant to drop to the correct 'All Right' position. The signal was on the same post as the East box up main advanced starter. When that signal was properly lowered, its counterbalance weight was raised high enough to release the 'slot' weight which controlled the movement of the Langley distant signal's counterweight. East box's up advanced starting signal was 603 yards from the signal box so, with Ted pulling the lever, the arm was rarely lowered correctly. So long as it was 'cocked' that would do for Ted. Unfortunately it would not do for the Langley/Chippenham 'slotting' arrangement at the foot of the post, and thus Langley Crossing's up distant was prevented from working properly and the latter signalman was given a lot of extra work.

He would heave over his distant signal lever, the duplex indicator would show 'Slot Off' but below

The view east from the London end of the down plaform at Chippenham, *circa* 1949, with a splendid early pattern GWR 'Backing' signal; the indicator below the arm gave three routes. In the middle distance is the Broad Gauge period goods shed, while on the left the Calne branch auto-trailer stands in the Calne Bay. On the sidings nearest the camera are a gassing tank and a horse-box. (*Courtesy Ray Thomas*)

wire so much that he could actually lift Chippenham East's counterbalance weight as he heaved with all his might on an overtight wire. No wonder then that poor old Ted Allen was not popular with his mates.

Although Chippenham East box was the larger of the two, and undoubtedly the busier job, Ray Thomas preferred, out of all the boxes he knew, to work in the snug, compact and very highly polished West box. The box was fairly low so that the signalman's eyes were level with the copper-capped chimney of a 'Castle', rather than the more usual signal box vantage which actually looked down on the trains.

West box provided a very fine vantage from which to admire the trains as one controlled them. Because it was on a high embankment, close to the main road through the town, there was also a view

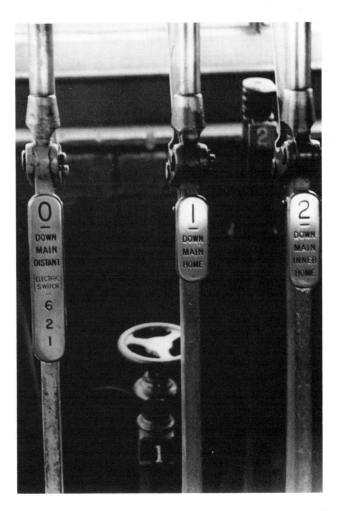

Lever brasses in Chippenham East box. Note the old pattern GWR wire adjuster (left) and the new type on the right. (*Courtesy Ray Thomas*)

that 'Signal Wrong'. He could slam his lever over as energetically as he liked — and it was a heavy pull — but he could not get his distant arm to lower to the correct angle. If he 'phoned Ted and asked him to wind in his advanced starter's wire so as to make the arm drop to the correct angle, Ted would make some excuse — 'I've already pulled my distant now, I can't move the starter' — and do nothing. As a result, express trains would brake ready to stop at Langley Crossing when they got the distant signal against them, and the innocent signalman at Langley would have to suffer the handsignals, none of which were in the rule book, and the indignant blowings of the whistle from irate footplatemen.

The only way to overcome this difficulty was for the Langley signalman to shorten the distant signal

A magnificent view of *Swansea Castle* glinting in the low evening sun outside Chippenham West box, Ray Thomas's favourite signal box, *circa* 1955. (*Courtesy Kenneth Leech*)

No 5056 *Earl of Powis* passing Chippenham at 86 mph on the down 'Bristolian' in October 1957, with Driver Shave at the regulator. (*Courtesy Kenneth Leech*)

over the buildings. On many evenings wonderful music came from the eight bells in the nearby church tower, more or less on a level with the box. When a 'King' or 'Castle'-hauled down express started out of the station, the loose-fitting, sliding windows of the box would shake in time with the mighty exhaust beat. Long trains, after stopping, would frequently have to draw up two or three coach lengths to bring the rear of the train on to the short platform, so there would be a double joy for the signalman for whom the engine was so close that he could have reached out and touched it.

When a down express such as the 1.15 pm Paddington or the 'Bristolian' went through non-stop, the air wave ahead of it used to make the windows crash inwards, a second before the front of the engine passed by, almost as if the train itself was hitting the box, but the most dramatic feature of all was when the campanologists were practising peals for an hour or more in the nearby tower. Then the clangorous pealing of the bells would mingle with the rhythmic, gun-shot blast of a 'King' or a 'Castle' Class engine starting out of Chippenham in a most exciting way.

The layout at West box was relatively simple but sufficient to be interesting. All the 17 levers were in use, unlike many boxes with large frames but where only the three or four signal levers at each end were in regular use and the remainder were only used when the local shunting trip arrived once a day. A lot of 'tail' traffic was taken off and put on to up passenger trains. In the morning and evening there were three up stopping passenger trains which terminated at Chippenham No 3 platform, and which then had to shunt into the down bay, Platform 2, for their return working. These were the 7.20 am Bradford-on-Avon which came via North Curve at Bradford Junction, the 7.6 am Frome auto and the 8.27 Trowbridge auto. There were also some interesting workings through to Calne: the 8 am Box auto, the 11.13 Trowbridge and the 12.55 Bristol to mention a few.

Auto-trains which terminated at Platform 3 did an easy shunt — into the Spur via points 11 and trap-point 7 and thence to the bay. Trains formed 'engine and coaches' were more difficult. The engine went up to East box and came back to West on the down main. It then reversed on to its train on the up main and pulled it back to the down main so as to be able to push it into the down bay.

Various relief signalmen were pleased to have Ray in the West box, but he was never invited in by the regular men who were, he was told, 'a funny, close lot'. One evening he went to the box at tea-time, by arrangement with a friendly reliefman, to work the box until the finish at 10 pm. He walked boldly up the steps and entered the box only to discover Percy, one of the regulars, was in possession. Ray, embarrassed to walk in uninvited, stammered that he had been expecting to see the reliefman. 'So was I,' replied Percy, 'but he's off sick, I've got to work my rest day and I'm not at all well either.'

Ray murmured his regrets and was just about to make his exit when Percy said: 'Aren't you Ray Thomas, the boy signalman?' Ray admitted he was.

'Do you think you could work this job for me for an hour?' asked Percy.

Ray said he could.

'Good lad,' said Percy, 'I feel proper poorly, I could do with a rest. If I'd have known I was going to end up feeling like this I wouldn't have come on at all. You give me a bit of a break at the frame and I'll sit here and do the booking.'

Ray said he would do the booking too, in pencil, so Percy sat back and after watching Ray for a while, fell asleep in the armchair.

Ray looked at the frame, the instruments and the train register to 'see what was about'. The signals were 'off' and 'Train on Line' pegged from Thingley Junction for the 4.35 Weston 'Merchant Venturer', and 'Line Clear' was pegged on the down line with the signals 'off' for the 4.15 pm Paddington. A few seconds later the up main approach track circuit dropped to 'Occupied'. Ray replaced the up distant signal to 'Caution' and sent 'on line' to East box. Seeing the tail lamp — it was the special 'Slip Coach' tail signal — he sent 2-1 to Thingley and 'unpegged', and was at once 'asked the road' for the 5.30 pm Westbury–Swindon semi-fast, running 'B' head-code, 3-1 on the bell.

As soon as the 'down London' cleared No 1 platform and 'Train out of Section' was sent to East box, at about 6.20 pm, East box 'asked the road' for a 3-1-3, the 6.33 Chippenham to Trowbridge auto. This was in fact 'empty stock', a small 'push-pull'-fitted tank engine sandwiched between two coaches. It had formed the 5.36 pm Calne auto to Chippenham, arriving at the bay platform at 5.48 pm, and had backed up the spur to come out on to the main line once the 'fast' was clear. This little train was signalled 1-3, Branch Passenger Train, to Thingley Junction. As soon as it had departed and the 2-1 had been sent to the East box, the bell at once rang out 2-3 for the engine of the 7.11 Chippenham–Westbury milk empties, the vehicles of which had been formed on Platform 3.

The engine came coasting down past the box and stopped clear of No 9 points. These were reversed, ground signal 10 was cleared and, with a quick 'toot', the engine backed gently over to its train. As soon as he had re-set the road, Ray gave 2-1 to East box and was at once 'asked the road' for the 5.5 Paddington, 4 bells, a 'hard-hitter'. The 6.33 Chippenham was still 'in block' to Thingley, so the only reply was to send 2-2-2, which East box refused. Two minutes later the 6.33 cleared Thingley, and Ray instantly offered '4 bells' which was accepted. He tapped out 4 beats to East box and heaved his own down line signals over while the East box man scrambled to do the same and get the distant signals 'off'. They 'dropped off' right in front of the 'fast' which shortly came pounding through at 80 mph, crashing the West box windows as it passed.

As he sent 'on line' to Thingley Junction and replaced the signals behind the train, Ray felt a large twinge of worry about what he was doing. Percy was 'dead to the world', and a 17-year-old trespasser was in charge of the box. Ought he to go on? He had gone through an evening shift frequently with Ted and others, but what if someone came in? But then, if he lost his courage and woke Percy from a deep sleep, would that make the man worse so that he would have to go home? As it was he would get £2 3s pay for working his rest day. Ray plucked up courage and decided to see the evening out.

He kept going through a busy sequence of trains, including one nerve-racking moment when he had to send the Station Pilot back to East box in the wrong direction — up the down line under a 4-2 bell code. Would the driver take a green light hand-signal from an unofficial signalman? In the near-darkness, the driver did not even notice who was holding the light and set off smartly back through the station. Percy woke up at 9.30 as the 7.50 pm Paddington set off for Bristol, blasting past the box in fine style. He felt a lot better for a really deep sleep and was astonished and grateful that Ray had run the entire service for him. All that remained to do was to deal with the Weymouth–Kensington milk train — which ran through non-stop — empty the ashes and sweep up ready for relief while Percy inked in the times Ray had marked faintly with pencil in the train register.

George arrived just before 10 and eyed Ray suspiciously. His temper was not improved after Percy related how Ray had done the job and 'saved my life'. He did not like the idea of a schoolboy being able to carry out such a skilful job, but of course he calculated without Ray's extensive experience and keen interest. From then on Ray was always welcome in the West box when Percy was on duty, and he became the only signalman to go to see and operate Ray's extensive model railway.

Month after month, Ray spent his spare time in the Chippenham boxes or somewhere around the district with one of his relief-signalman friends, but about 12 months after the incident related above, Chippenham got a new Station Master, a Scot. The men were in any case suspicious of a 'foreigner', and he did not ease his entry into the small world of Chippenham's railway by visiting signal boxes at 3 in the morning to try and catch men having a nap during a quiet spell in order to get through the tiring night shift.

Such behaviour was always, since the days of lineside policemen, considered a sneaky, 'below the belt' way to act, tantamount to saying that you did not trust your men — an insult — which made for a great deal of indignation. Poor old Jock was soon known derisively as 'old Worry-guts' and their derision soon knew no bounds when the interloper was heard to speak slightingly of the GWR ATC (Automatic Train Control). Now, the ATC was one of *the* most sacred and beloved of GWR institutions amongst all grades. Signalmen revered it quite as much as enginemen, so you can imagine that the poor old Station Master's reputation was at rock bottom as the word went round that 'Old Worry-guts doesn't think the ATC is safe.'

Ray was on Chippenham platform one afternoon when the Station Master saw him and walked up. 'I hope I never see you in either of these boxes again,' he said, and walked away. After that, Ray never visited either box although he did carry on working in the more outlying places like Langley Crossing, but soon even that came to an end when he was conscripted into the army. He never saw the Chippenham boxes again, but they remain crystal clear in his memory and the recollections of those six wonderful years cannot be taken away.

So it is with all of us who knew and loved the steam-hauled, semaphore-signalled railway — wherever that might have been. It was a special way of life and I and many others feel very loyal to it.

I hope this book will enable the younger enthusiast to understand and to share my feelings, and will bring back happy memories for those already 'in the know'.

This happy group of 'spotters' was photographed by Les Reason in about 1936 at Langley (Bucks) at the end of a cycle ride from Watford. The engine is No 2935 *Caynham Court*, with experimental poppet valves, working a 'B' headcode passenger train on the down relief line.

And this is how it all began for so many of us — at the lineside, falling in love with magnificent machines, fine engineering, good architecture and good company. All these lads are still alive and well and still good friends 55 years on. (*Les Reason*)

Above left The original LSWR signal box at Dean, between Salisbury and Romsey, in 1974. This building had stood here since 1875 although over the years it had lost its decorative valancing and other decorative timberwork. It housed a 17-lever frame augmented by draw-slides 18-20 as from 13 August 1972. The nearest signal post appears to be an LSWR lattice-work production. A very similar mast with a lower quadrant arm stood in this position in 1890. This ancient scene was swept away on 9 September 1980.

Left St Mary's Crossing signal box, dating from about 1875 when block signalling was installed, and apparently unchanged since then. The old lamp also looks as if it is original. The line here is climbing at 1 in 75 from the Severn valley near Gloucester to Sapperton tunnel, piercing the Cotswold ridge and giving access to the valley of the Upper Thames. Down the path to the left is the derelict Thames–Severn canal with a magnificent, stone-built mill on the waterside. A peaceful place to sit in the grass and await the passage of some very hard-working locomotives. Photographed in August 1964.

Above Or perhaps sitting on the hot, peaceful, sunny platform at Cornwood, the 1890-vintage signal box emitting occasional pleasant sounds, one could relax, soak up the scene and every few minutes have one's peace most agreeably shattered by the sound of speeding steam, in this case a 'Castle' on the down 'Cornishman', or steam working hard 'in the collar' if it was an up train. (*Peter Barlow/Author's Collection*)

Above Another fine sunny day for sitting in the bracken and watching other men work! Collett 0-6-2T No 5636 and a colleague perform manoeuvres outside Grovesend Colliery Loop signal box. This is the classic GWR signal box design, erected here in 1911 and opened in 1912 as part of the GWR's Swansea avoiding line, otherwise known as the 'Swansea District line'. (*Peter Barlow/Author's Collection*)

Above right Utter silence at Abbeyfeale station, in the wilds of County Kerry — nothing but billowing clouds and crying curlews. The Saxby & Farmer signal seems to be peeping over the wall to see what I am up to with my camera. Photographed in 1974.

Right Bucolic bliss at grassy, flower-strewn West Meon station in 1949, where even the 1903 vintage signal box is disappearing under a heavy growth of ivy. The Meon Valley line ran through some of the most beautiful countryside in Southern England from Alton to Fareham. What a delight it is to the eye of a connoisseur of railways — and what a commercial disaster it must have been. (*Author's Collection*)

Above The Banbury–Chipping Norton auto-car has arrived at the outer end of its journey across the high, remote Cotswolds, having passed gingerly over Hook Norton viaduct — which was probably felt to sway as the load rolled across — past a neolithic stone circle at Great Rollright and through a couple of tunnels. The '37xx' tank engine has berthed the coach in the return platform and is now parked, prior to 'running round', whilst its crew pursue that all-important railway business – making tea. The signal box is a contactor's production — Gloucester Carriage & Wagon Co — and the signalman's bike leans outside. This is very hilly country for cycling. The year is 1954. (*Peter Barlow/Author's Collection*)

Right Looking down on to the Stroud end of the short tunnel at Sapperton. There is a delicious feeling of awe about tunnels, especially this one, hacked through the Cotswold rock. It exudes a fearsome feeling of power when one looks into the gloomy, craggy cutting and the huge, black mouth, perhaps a residue from the energy expended by hundreds of sweating, struggling navvies back in the 1840s. The short tunnel was approximately 325 yards long, the long tunnel about 1 mile. The signal is Sapperton's up main distant with two 'banner repeaters'. The signal was provided in this form owing to the abrupt change of gradient at this point. An up train (left-hand track) was on a 1 in 58 rising grade which changed to 1 in 94 falling in this cutting. If the distant signal was, as here, at 'Caution', the driver could tell from the repeaters whether he was expected to stop dead at the home signal or continue into the goods loop. The alternative to this would have been a 'splitting' distant, routing to the left-hand divergence (see page 69).

Distant views. *Above far left* Seen from a road bridge on a foggy day is a rear view of Dorrington's up distant signal on a rather battered concrete post. The circular, grey box is a London Midland Region detector for sending an indication of the position of the arm back to the repeater in the signal box. The large, black quadrant is the rear of a 'sighting plate', the face of which is white. Note that the signal's cast-iron finial has lost the top half of its spike. Photographed in 1977.

Above left Codford's and Upton Lovell Crossing's down distant signal in 1974, the single arm covering both locations. The fine GWR arm with old-style spectacle plate is mounted on a wooden mast, and the arm is worked by a motor at the base of the post. The ball of any distant signal's finial was painted yellow, but if the finial was on a post carrying both 'Danger' and 'Distant' signals, the ball was painted red.

Far left A Great Northern Railway-style 'somersault' distant signal on the up line approaching Havenhouse on the Skegness–Boston line. The post is LNER concrete and the arm was LNER corrugated steel until about 1983 when it and several others in the area were replaced by *wooden* arms which might have been newly made or might have been ex-Great Northern Railway — a fascinating little mystery. Perhaps there is a railway-loving S&T Inspector somewhere in the Fens! Photographed in 1984.

Left On the GWR's 'New Line' to Birmingham, Bicester's down main distant sports a rather 'do it yourself'-style lower arm in this 1955 view. The latter is the 'slipping distant', worked by the main arm's down-rod, for the benefit of the guard of Bicester's slip coach service off the 5.10 pm Paddington–Birmingham express. (*Peter Barlow/Author's Collection*)

Stop signals. *Above* A classic GWR stop arm mounted on a concrete post with a sighting plate and a 'track circuit' diamond, which releases the fireman of a train standing at this signal from the obligation under Rule 55 of walking to the signal box to remind the signalman of the presence of his train. Torquay up home signal, 1978.

Above Elstree, LMR, in 1975, looking south, with a Leicester-bound express and arms raised for all four tracks.

Left I was enjoying a sunny stroll around the layout at Taunton East Junction in 1971 when I took this photograph of a BR(WR) tubular steel signal with a 3-foot arm controlling egress from the up goods avoiding line to the up main line.

Right Coming back from photographing No 4498 at Danby Wiske in 1968, I saw this North Eastern Railway lattice post signal on the Catterick Camp railway. I was unable to take the front view as I would have been 'into the sun'.

Below The Southern hit on a very happy idea when it decided to make signal masts out of old rails. They are standardised, cheap yet characterful, especially with the old corrugated arm. Where else but Corfe Castle, in 1965.

Above far left A lattice mast by Saxby & Farmer Ltd. The ancient arm could not manage to creak down any further than this as it was getting stiff from lack of use. Taken at Gort, Co Galway, in 1982.

Above left Also at Gort, a Saxby & Farmer swivelling ground signal. The rod on the right is driven by the moving point blades and turns the red lamp off, bringing the white light into view.

Far left The Great Western Railway is not one that springs to mind when 'somersault' signals are mentioned, but with the takeover by the GWR in 1921–3 of the Barry, Brecon & Merthyr, Cardiff, Rhymney and Taff Vale Railways, the GWR had more somersault signals than any other company in Britain — after the LNER. This somersault signal was photographed at Barry in 1952. (*Author's Collection*)

Left As lonely a place as any in England. Twin GWR stop signals make the down home and up starter for Tidworth station, viewed towards Ludgershall in 1951. (*Author's Collection*)

Above Six arms on one post — well, almost. This splendid 'Christmas tree' signal at Henley-on-Thames sports a classic stop signal as the down home with a 'Calling on' arm beneath, and three 'symmetrically balanced' arms below that, two for the down line into the station and one for the up line, and finally another standard arm, with its back to us, also for the up line. The signal box is a fine example of the GWR standard design in use from 1890-1901 and was photographed in 1954. (*Peter Barlow/Author's Collection*)

Above left I really enjoyed this friendly little signal standing so proudly on the platform at Aberystwyth in 1981. It was nice to be able to look it 'straight in the eye', especially when it happened to be genuine GWR with a 'wasp-waist' spectacle. The rear view shows the whole handsome design to the best advantage. There must be an enthusiastic S&T technician at Aberystwyth — perhaps he will slip some proper black paint on to the butt-end instead of that insipid grey.

Left Back in steam days, looking off a bridge towards Tiverton station; the line from Dulverton passes under the bridge, while that from Tiverton Junction crosses the middle of the view. The nearest signal has a 4-foot arm with a 3-foot 'Shunt' arm below, the 'S' on the arm appearing here like an ellipse. Facing us is a very tall signal with a 5-foot top arm and a finial carrying a pulley over which passes the chain which raises and lowers the lamp and thus saves the 'lampie' the dangerous job of climbing to the top of the post. There is a duplicate arm below made in the special form which indicates that it is a 'duplex', or repeating, arm. Photograph taken *circa* 1955. (*Author's Collection*)

Above Branch lines off branch lines here. The nearest track with the ringed 3-foot arm comes from the Royal Naval depot at Trecwn, while at the higher level is the Clynderwen/Rosebush to Letterston Junction branch. Note the motor-worked trap points. The view is towards Letterston Junction, on the Whitland–Fishguard line in the depths of Pembrokeshire, and was taken in 1955. (*Peter Barlow/Author's Collection*)

Above The Midland Railway signal box at Manton Junction in 1983. The stumpy signal is on the Peterborough branch (now the main line, I suppose), and the train has just joined the old MR main line from Kettering to Nottingham and the North.

Above right The Isle of Wight railways were among the most splendid for efficiency, morale and 'atmosphere' in Britain. Here on Ryde Pier in 1959 is an ex-LSWR lattice mast with its BR(SR) arm raised and the platform indicator routing to '2'. About to tie up at the pier is that marvellous old paddle-steamer for a ride on which we would wait an extra couple of hours. The engine, *Calbourne*, is about to 'run round' the empty coaches prior to pushing them into the platform ready for the hordes of holidaymakers about to disembark.

Right A very stately example of a Southern 'old rails' signal at Swanley in 1957. Corrugated Southern Railway arms and a red 'S' on the 'Shunt' signal make this a splendid beast, full of individuality. The distant signal arm acts as a repeater for an automatic semaphore stop signal further down the line. (*Peter Barlow/Author's Collection*)

Above far left A juvenile LMS signal, finding it difficult to raise its as yet half-grown arms at Workington, Cumbria, in 1989. (*Kevin Connolly/Author's Collection*)

Above left Great Western Railway 'symmetrically balanced' signals at Worcester Shrub Hill station in 1973 — the Station box up platform line starting with Wylds Lane distant beneath it. The incoming 'Midland' diesel on a Bristol–Birmingham train has come off the LMR at Abbott's Wood Junction and joined the WR at Norton Junction and, as a 'foreigner', adds a taste of 'inter-company', harking back to steam days when Shrub Hill was a GWR/LMS Joint station.

Left Atlas having departed, the fine old GWR signal box, with a frame of 70 levers numbered 1-84, looks as good as new. Enough tradition remains here from the steam past to imagine the splendid procession of locomotives and rolling-stock which used once to come through the Joint station: Midland 4-4-0 express engines and outside framed 2-4-0s, 'Jubilees' and 'Class 5s', GWR 'single-wheelers', 'Cities', 'Stars' and 'Bulldogs', to name but a very few. The broad tracks and the signals are handsome, but there is also an emptiness — a steam engine is required!

Above In the summer of 1975 I was about to go and live in Ireland so I made the effort to do what I had put off for years — to go and photograph the North London Railway, that elusive line that rode on bridges, cutting across all the great main lines and winding its way secretively around the rickety roof-tops and crumbling back garden walls of London's densest suburbs. Dalston Junction was just one of many places where lines wandered off under houses or over the roof-tops to — where? Ah! That was the fun of railways — where did that old line end up? The tracks in the foreground have come from Poplar and the view is towards Broad Street terminus. This box was built by the North London Railway and opened in 1871; luckily for us it still retained its original valancing in 1975. The lever frame within seemed to be of LNWR manufacture but was in fact a North London Railway, Bow Works, design, locked by that company's tappet system under the floor.

Above left Photographed earlier at Dalston Junction in 1955 were these symmetrically balanced signals, on the Richmond-bound line. The distant signal is for Dalston Western Junction. (*Peter Barlow/Author's Collection*)

More symmetrically balanced arms. *Left* At Droitwich Junction, 6 miles north of Worcester, the Midland Railway took its own track, to the right, to regain the Birmingham–Bristol line at Stoke Priors Junction, while the GWR bore away to the left for Kidderminster and Wolverhampton. The signal box, a classic red brick and hip roof job, is in the 'V' of the junction with the actual junction signal somewhat masked by a single post, up line signal. The rather splendid BR(WR) bracket signal with GWR-style symmetrically balanced arms routes to the down main (right-hand arm) and from the down main to the goods loop. An old-fashioned view — but taken in 1983.

Above The earlier GWR method of dealing with the same type of signal. This is Didcot West End's down relief line home and down relief to down Oxford branch. Coming in on the up relief line is one reason why it was such fun to work on the Didcot–Swindon section — one of three 'running-in' turns for ex-Works engines. In this case it's the 10.55 am Swindon–Didcot local with No 4037 *South Wales Borderers*. No 4037 will probably work back on a Banbury–Stoke Gifford 'H' goods as far as Swindon. Photographed in 1955. (*Author's Collection*)

Above No 1450 arriving at Bourne End with an auto-train from Maidenhead in 1956. As the train is a 'push-pull' the driver is running with a tail lamp at each end, hence what appears to be a 'G' headcode on the engine. In January 1956 the layout at Bourne End was simplified to abolish the old South box and put all the work on to North box. The ground disc on the bracket on the right was then elevated, making centre-pivot arms necessary to provide clearance. The highest arm routes to Maidenhead, the lower to Marlow and the disc to sidings. The lone signal is the Bay to Branch starting. (*Les Reason/Author's Collection*)

Above right The London & South Western Railway's initials — LSWR — might be interpreted as standing for 'latticework railway'. This very handsome ensemble, photographed in 1974, was the 'splitting' or 'directing' distant signals for the Eastleigh/Southampton junction a mile ahead at Romsey; the arm is raised for the Southampton direction. Although the arms are of BR(SR) origin, the signal masts are almost certainly LSWR and would once have carried lower quadrant arms.

Right Another splitting distant, and this BR(WR) example was very unusual and possibly unique because the arm seen lowered to 'All Right' routed to the dead-end sidings of Chelsea Basin — the Thames was beyond the buffer stops. Since the Aylesbury smash of 1904 it had been the practice to fix distant signals at 'Caution' when approaching a dead-end, but in rare instances drivers' difficulties with changing gradients obliged a departure from the rule. The signal arrangement at Sapperton (see page 53) would have been a better solution to the problem here since the driver would then have had the distant at 'Caution', and warning of his route would have been conveyed by the banner repeater. Photographed in 1974.

Splitting stop signals. *Above far left* Lattice 'dolls' and an 'old rails' mast provide the junction signal at Worgret, in 1965. The left-hand arm is for the Swanage branch.

Above left LSWR latticework with the 'proper' arms on the 'Up Platform' and 'Up Fast' lines at Seaton Junction, Devon, in 1951. (*Author's Collection*)

Left A busy moment at St Erth in 1973 with the St Ives branch signal lowered on the very handsome BR(WR) tubular steel bracket signal. The Class '52' diesel is going to collect milk tankers from the yard to form the 14.45 to Kensington, while a down express from Paddington is arriving in the distance.

Above The 'company' atmosphere survived for years after nationalisation, and here at Gerrard's Cross the 'GWR/LNER Joint line' flavour remains strong in 1955. The view shows the GWR timber bracket signal on the down main with the 'Down Main to Down Platform Line' home signal bowing to an ex-LNER 'L1' Class 2-6-4 tank hauling some Gresley coaches on a Marylebone–Aylesbury, via Princes Risborough, train. (*Peter Barlow/Author's Collection*)

Above far left A lovely May day — 'the fairest that ever was seen' — and what better place to spend it than beside the tracks in company with venerable signals, trees in fresh green leaf, and wild flowers, at Gort, Co Galway, in 1981. This old Saxby & Farmer signal still carries its original arm but is fitted with a CIE fluorescent red plate which, luckily, had been considerably weathered by the Atlantic storms. Fitted to the post is a typical CIE tubular bracket with one of their arms, bent horizontally for stiffness. It's an oddly unbalanced design, yet after a while one gets used to it and notices how the CIE designer has tried to keep the job tidy by using on the new all-metal arm a spectacle plate similar to that on the old arm. The cap on the metal post is more expensively made than need be to keep it in sympathy with the old S&F wooden cap. A lovely, sylvan scene.

Above left A rear view of the same signal showing the white 'blinkers' which move to cover the 'back lights' of the signal lamps to prove to the signalman that the arm has answered the lever.

Left Signal metamorphosis — a good example of the evolutionary, rather than revolutionary, changes which were once the norm on our railways. These venerable wooden signals at Cowes in 1929 must surely date back to the introduction of signalling there in 1875. The signal box seen here replaced the original and dates from 1892. It had a 22-lever frame. (*Dr Jack Hollick/Author's Collection*)

Above Evolution — the Southern Railway's replacement for the wooden bracket signal at Cowes, seen in 1959. Drifting steam from the engine slightly obscures the right-hand 'doll'. Apart from details of signal construction, the scene at Cowes station has changed not at all since 1929, or even 1909 — which was a large part of its charm, and the charm of railways generally.

A signal's career. *Above left* This GWR wooden bracket signal has 5-foot-long arms; the top arm is the Wolvercote Sidings down main starting signal, with the down main and branch 'directing', 'routing' or 'splitting' distants for the box in advance, Wolvercote Junction — the Worcester line distant is lowered. The engine is a 1910-vintage 'Star' and its seven-coach train consists of modern GWR stock. The date is 1929. (*Dr Jack Hollick/Author's Collection*)

Left The view from the same bridge 25 years later. The signal, this time with the Birmingham line distant arm lowered, has the same formation but is a GWR 1942 tubular steel production, erected during wartime re-signalling when the down goods running loop was laid. The curious old sidings, which had been in use since at least as early as 1880, intended for hay and cattle loading, are still in use in 1954. The engine, No 6976 *Graythwaite Hall*, built in 1947, is somewhat grimy but like the 'Star' is hauling the latest coaches, all BR except for an LNER Gresley restaurant car third from the engine. (*Peter Barlow/Author's Collection*)

This page above left After the closure of Wolvercote Sidings and the associated signal box on 9 June 1958, the stop arm was removed, leaving only the Junction box's directing distant signals. The goods loop behind the signal is still in use in this 1968 view, but was abolished in 1973.

Above right The LNWR's cheap alternative to a bracket signal — splitting distants for Perry Barr North Junction below the starting signal for Great Barr, Birmingham, dual masts braced together by a single steel rod. Tough, rough 'n' ready, and practical — they sum up the entire LNWR ethos for me. Photographed in 1955. (*Peter Barlow/Author's Collection*)

Above left Latticework strength with elegance on 'the Southern' — Salisbury East's up main starting signal, a BR(SR) arm, above Salisbury Tunnel Junction's splitting distants, Southern Railway corrugated arms for Waterloo/Southampton; the Southampton arm is raised in this 1972 view. Signalling at Salisbury (SR) used the American Pneumatic Railway Signal Company's system, built under licence by the British Pneumatic Railway Signal Co, a subsidiary of Westinghouse of Chippenham (Wilts) at whose factory the equipment was made. The system was introduced to the LSWR in 1901 at Grateley near Salisbury and was installed at Salisbury in 1902 (see page 167ff). Compressed air is admitted into the cylinder and drives a piston which is connected to a lever to raise the signal arm. The cylinder for the stop signal is clearly silhouetted against the sky.

Above right This very unusual — but not unique — arrangement of distant signals on the up fast line at Kentish Town, photographed in 1957, is the result of 'signal sighting' conditions. Smoke and/or fog in this confined space made the stop signal ahead invisible at times, so the topmost distant signal was used as a 'repeater' for the aspect of Islip Street signal box home signal about 50 yards ahead. The arm below this is the up fast line distant signal for St Paul's Road Passenger Junction box up fast home signal, while the left-hand distant arm directs trains 'down the hole' at the latter box to Moorgate station. Islip Street box was demolished on 23 December 1966 when an empty stock train was derailed and damaged it. Shortly afterwards an up local dmu passenger train ran into the wreckage, killing about five people and demolishing the box. (*Peter Barlow/Author's Collection*)

Right A fine old survivor on the down fast line at Kentish Town Junction in 1957 — a Midland Railway wooden bracket signal, pickled in sulphur, and dating back to the days when Mr Johnson's gleaming, crimson-painted 'single-wheelers' came flying through here, and when the signals were a properly maintained white. The last vestige of paint has long since departed from this old warrior. The distant signal arm is worked from Carlton Road Junction by an electric motor fixed low down on the right of the main mast. The left-hand stop signal routes trains 'over the top' to Highgate Junction. (*Peter Barlow/Author's Collection*)

Above left Back on the 'latticework railway', a superb example of the style at St Denys, where the Portsmouth line forks away from the line to London, about 2 miles north of Southampton. The track is quadruple, the 'Local' and 'Through' lines from Southampton merging into double track from St Denys. The signals are correspondingly arranged in two pairs, the left-hand of each pair routing to the up main (London), the right-hand of each pair to the branch. The arm raised is 'Up Through to Up Main', and the year is 1973.

Left Another way of arranging junction signals. This very handsome LSWR lattice bracket controls the exit from Bevois Park yard, on the up side of the line adjacent to the signal in the previous picture. It stands between No 1 Reception Line on the left and No 2 Reception Line on the right, the left-hand and right-hand 'dolls' applying to their respective lines. The two top arms route trains to the up main and the lower arms to the Portsmouth direction. The upper quadrant arms are made more pleasing to the eye by the old Southern Railway corrugation technique. Both this and the signal in the previous photograph once carried LSWR lower-quadrant arms.

This page above left The LSWR-pattern up main home (higher arm) and up main to branch home signals at Evercreech Junction North in 1965. Below is a ringed-arm 'Shunt' signal used, for instance, to call the bank engine to the rear of a freight train requiring assistance on the tortuous climb of the Mendips to Masbury summit on the way to Radstock and Bath. Note that whilst the Southern Railway signal engineer found it necessary to replace the original wooden main mast with one of his 'old rail' masts, he kindly retained the original finials, the short wooden post and the ornate spandrel casting.

Above right This strange old fellow, also at Evercreech, is an LSWR-pattern 'Backing' signal which routed movements from the down main to the up main or up sidings or down branch or up branch. Here too the SR engineer has been obliged to replace the wooden main mast but has been careful to retain the essential flavour of this splendid old signal. Dare I suggest that he had actual sympathy for these grand old specimens and wanted to preserve them? In the background is Evercreech Junction North box, erected in about February 1886 when the line to Bath was doubled.

Above far left Southern Railway signals at Cuxton, Kent, in 1984, with a Southern Railway arm routing into the loop. The distant signal was worked from Wickham Sidings box until about 1971, and is seen here as a repeater for a three-aspect colour signal ahead. A nice stumpy signal, placed low enough to be able to see the 'works' clearly.

Above left Southern Railway signals on a foggy day in the south London suburbs at Tulse Hill. The signal applies to the left-hand track but is sited on the 'wrong' side of the line due to track curvature. The left-hand Southern Railway pattern arm is the down platform line starting signal routing trains to Streatham, and below it a three-aspect colour-light forms Streatham's distant signal. When the semaphore arm is at 'Danger', the latter shows no light, but when the arm is raised the colour-light displays — according to conditions at Streatham and beyond — yellow, double yellow or green. The right-hand arms route to Streatham Hill and Clapham Junction, the distant signal being that for Leigham Junction. Below that there is a 'Warning Acceptance' arm, white with horizontal red borders, and to one side is a small indicator which produces the letter 'W' when the arm is raised.

Left This seems to me to be a hybrid signal design dating from 1923 when the MR, LNWR and many lesser companies were grouped into the London Midland & Scottish Railway. The method of construction and the parts used suggest a marriage of MR and LNWR practice, and similar construction was used in BR(LMR) days on a signal at Grayrigg. Could it be that immediately post-grouping designs were still current *circa* 1952? The signal was photographed at Carnforth East Junction in 1986 on the old Midland Railway route from Hellifield. The arm is raised for a train to run into Carnforth station on the West Coast Main Line, while the tracks ahead are ex-Furness Railway and lead to Ulverstone, Barrow, Whitehaven and Carlisle.

Above This is where the dark green Drummond 'T9' 4-4-0 with its curiously liveried coaches — salmon pink upper panels and chocolate below — met the green, Indian red, brass and copper-laden 4-4-0 and sensible crimson lake coaches of the Great Western, or where the Bulleid 'Pacific' set out with spinning wheels at the head of seven coaches, banked in the rear by three diminutive tank engines, for Exeter Central, another seven coaches, and Waterloo. For this is the 'Down Homes' gantry of Exeter St David's West box in 1971. The top left-hand arm routes from 'Down Main to Southern', the middle arm is 'Down Main', with a 'Calling on' arm below, and the other is 'Down Middle to Southern'. The supporting mast is on No 1 down platform with the old South Devon Railway carriage shed behind, which probably dated back to the days of the atmospheric railway. Curving around the shed from the down platform are the 'South Devon sidings'. The route to Waterloo is at the extreme right of the view.

Above far left A closer view of the signals at the left-hand end of the Exeter gantry. The 'Down Platform No 1 to Down Main' arm is lowered. Below it is a red and white striped 'Calling on' arm, and to the left is an ancient GWR 'subsidiary' signal routing to the South Devon sidings. The single post and arm beyond controls the exit from those sidings, and beyond that Southern Region rails cross the WR main line in front of Exeter West box. There was no access to the Southern from No 1 platform; 'Up Southern' trains used Platform 3, and 'Down Southerns' used Platform 4, the opposite face of the central island platform, which they shared with WR trains. Exeter St David's was a cramped place and difficult for the signalmen to operate but they worked it with great skill born of years of experience. Except on Summer Saturdays or other seasonal peaks, the 117-lever West box (numbered to 131) was worked by one signalman with a boy for the train register and telephones. Happily, West box has been preserved complete and will be re-erected.

Above left The Great Western used 32-inch diameter elevated discs — known to staff as 'banjos' — as 'running signals' at Worcester and Gloucester in preference to the more usual 'centre pivot' semaphore in this restricted clearance situation. The 'CO' ('Calling on') discs are standard GWR 16-inch diameter examples. The practice of large discs for running signals was rare, the only other examples known to me being at Keyham, Plymouth, and at Hallatrow, Somerset, as the junction signals for the Bristol/Limpley Stoke divergence. The discs here at Worcester station were arranged as 'junction signals', but at Gloucester a single large disc worked with a route indicator to give direction. The discs in the photograph were operated from Worcester Station box and formed the 'Up Platform Line' (left-hand) and 'Up Platform to Up Middle' home signals. The 'Calling on' discs indicated to the driver of a train that the line was clear only to the rear of a stationary train ahead. This arrangement was useful when bringing the station shunting engine to the rear of a train, or when coupling two trains together.

Trios. *Left* The LSWR latticework steel signals were simultaneously elegant and functional and, I feel, make the GWR's wooden signals look 'home-made'. This very fine bracket carries Salisbury East's down homes, all still with ex-Southern Railway arms, and is viewed looking towards Tunnel Junction in 1972.

Above How, I wonder, would the 'latticework railway' have handled this situation at Blaenau Ffestiniog, where the signals have been entrenched in the cutting side? It is a splendid signal, most enjoyable, but it does look — dare I say it? — amateurish! Note the mark of the ring once carried by the left-hand arm. A 1957 view. (*Peter Barlow/Author's Collection*)

Above left This is a nostalgic view for me, as I spent much of my schooldays here, and is full of the sort of detail which gave the railway its fascination — there was so much going on. Reading West Main's up relief line home signals carry a slipping distant, motor operated from Reading East Main (I wonder how often an express slipped a coach on the up relief line?). The arms read, from left to right: to Up Goods Running Loop; Up Relief; Up Relief to Up Main. On the left is the timber yard and sawmill of the GWR Signal Works, where all those handsomely tapered wooden signal posts were made from tree trunks. Note the 'Vaughan' crane on its overhead gantry for log handling, and close by a well-cared-for vintage coach in S&T Department service, a very old signal, and the 1890 vintage Reading Goods Lines West box. Photographed in 1957. (*Peter Barlow/Author's Collection*)

Left Reading West Main's up 'Berks & Hants' line home signals with outer distant signals worked from East Main. From the left, top row, the arms route to: Up Relief Line (Platform 10); Up Bay (Platform 7); Up Main; Up Bays (Platforms 1, 2, and 3). The left-hand distant arm applies to trains going to the up relief line, and both distants are placed low so that the slip coach guard can see them easily and know whether it will be safe to slip his coach. Only if the distant signal was lowered would he pull the slipping lever; he would not slip if the main part of the train was going to be stopped in case his free-wheeling coach collided with it. Note the ringed arm signal on the left, controlling the exit from the engine shed, and the old-type 'Backing' signal on the extreme right. Both signals carry an indicator which displays stencilled letters advising the driver of his route; the former clearly has four stencils. Reading Goods Lines West box can be seen and a 'Castle' Class engine dips down the slope to the depot in this 1955 view. (*Peter Barlow/Author's Collection*)

Above Drivers of up WR trains approaching Exeter met this fine fellow dominating the sky by the Exe bridge, but having taken their route from it they then had to remember to look out for a relatively obscure ground disc signal, one in a bank of three, on the far side of the bridge. This signal was erected in 1925 on a single post with four 'dolls', and was enlarged to this form in March 1940, with the addition of the left-hand 'doll'. From the left the arms route to: Locomotive Depot; Up Goods Running Loop; Platform 6 (Up Relief Line); Platform 5 (Up Main); Platform 4 (Up Middle). The distant signals belong to Exeter Middle box, but only the up main distant is operable. Photographed in 1971.

This little-known place on the 'dark side' of Didcot was the haunt of pannier tanks with 'spark arrester' chimneys like something out of a Wild West movie. As a boy I used to see these engines reversing out of Didcot yard, up to the North Junction, pushing a shunters' 'gig' — on which were riding a couple of shunters — and a goodly raft of vans behind. The train was heading for this place, the entrance to the Didcot Ordnance Depot, off the West Curve.

In 1953 there were two engines booked to work in the Depot 12 hours a day, five days a week, and one worked there on Saturday morning as well. The area is now a caravan park and an electricity generating station, but the narrow bridge seen here in 1954 in these two views looking towards Foxhall Junction and the Bristol/South Wales main line, is still in place. When you next visit the Great Western Society at Didcot, park safely, go and look over the fence and count the differences between 1955 and 1991.

In the picture above, the left-hand arm is Foxhall Junction's home signal, while the three smaller arms are worked from the Depot ground frame. Only the middle of the three was slotted by Foxhall — why the others were not is something of a mystery. The facing and trailing points into and out of the depot can be seen together with a ground signal for a reversing movement into the Depot from the right-hand track.

Notice the 'switch diamond' junction in the view opposite, normally associated with relatively high-speed main-line turn-outs where a continuous rail surface is presented to wheels for safety's sake. Here the device is used, in spite of a 10 mph speed restriction, because of the need to bring a workmen's train into the depot each day from Oxford over the exceptionally sharply curved junction. There was an unscheduled number of freight workings and

during the war the place would, doubtless, have been very busy.

The Foxhall Junction signalman pulled the facing point bolt and facing point and the bolts and points of the moveable diamonds. This took six lever movements, six terrific heaves. His signal box was on the main line (it can just be seen behind the finial of the depot exit signal in the photograph), a long way from the points. Think of the weight of rodding he had to move and the friction in it as it came around the inside of the curve, crossed under the rails via two sets of bell cranks and then towards the camera on the outside of the curve.

The various points and point bolts beyond the West Curve double track were operated from a ground frame inside the depot but the ground frame levers were locked until released by the Foxhall Junction signalman pulling lever No 13. The signal controlling the exit from the depot was worked from the ground frame but the arm was also controlled — or 'slotted' — by a lever in Foxhall Junction, because lowering this signal also allowed the train to enter Didcot North Junction's section. Therefore the slotting lever in Foxhall Junction was electrically locked with the 'Line Clear' indication from North Junction.

Because of the divided control of the signalling, very great co-operation was required between the Depot Inspector and the signalmen at Foxhall and Didcot North Junctions in giving advice of trains approaching for the depot and in informing the Foxhall signalman when a train was clear inside, off the West Curve, complete with tail lamp. The bracket signal, facing points and moveable diamond were taken out of use in October 1959, and the trailing point was removed in 1963. (*Peter Barlow/Author's Collection*)

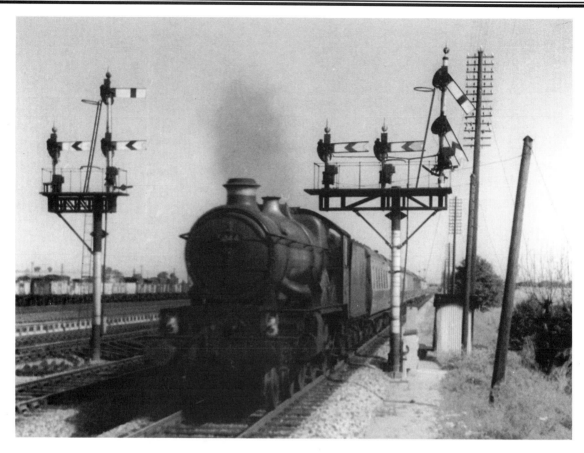

Above left Far away both in atmosphere and distance from the hidden West Curve, here are the quadruple track eastern approaches to Didcot on the London–Bristol/Gloucester/South Wales line at Moreton Cutting in 1954. No 5044 *Earl of Dunraven* comes down the main line very fast with a light grey smoke indicating a very hot fire. The engine is passing Moreton Cutting's down main advanced starting signal with Didcot East Junction's outer distant below. The central distant signal on that bracket is East Junction's 'Down Main to Down Relief Line' directing signal and the left-hand arm as we look at it routes 'Down Main to Down Avoiding Line'. Behind the down relief line signal is the crowded Moreton Cutting yard, full of coal and general merchandise for London and the Southern Region. The latter's engines bringing traffic here worked 'light' to Didcot to turn on the triangle, adding to the signalmen's work — 'Another Southern donkey to turn' — and adding to the pleasure of being a 'locospotter' on those windy platforms. (*Les Reason*)

Left Non-GWR signals on GWR posts over the up relief and up through lines at Newton Abbot in 1971. We are looking towards Newton Abbot East box and the signals are Newton Abbot West's up through line starter (on the left) beside the empty post which once carried the 'Up Through to Up Relief Line' starter when there was a junction here. The third signal routes 'Up Relief to Up Through' over the crossover, half of the original 'scissors' junction, and then there is the up relief line starter. The distant signals are worked from East box, the 'Calling on' arms from the West. These are all electrically operated Westinghouse signals installed in 1927 when the station was rebuilt. Note that the electric motors work the arms directly — there are no 'down-rods'.

Above A splendid array of BR(WR) semaphores, looking east from Taunton station in 1971 with the East Junction box on the right. The signals are worked from that box and apply, from the left, to: Up Relief Line starting; Up Main to Up Relief; Up Main; Down Main starting; Down Main to Down Relief line; Down Relief Line starting. The distant signals are worked from Taunton West Station box.

Above left One of the best remembered scenes from my schooldays — looking west off the end of Platform 2 at Reading in 1954. No 76016 is in Platform 3 with a Southern working to Southampton, and a 'Hall' can just be seen waiting on Platform 1 with a 'Berks & Hants' line train. Southern engines, ex-Eastleigh Works, called routinely in these bays and I have vivid memories of several ex-LB&SCR 'Atlantic' types standing here. All the 'Remembrance' Class 4-6-0s worked in here as well as 'King Arthur' Class engines, 'T9' 4-4-0s and 'M7' 0-4-4 tanks. The combinations of 'Southern' and 'Western' were splendid — especially as the ex-GWR diesel railcars also worked out of the bays to Hungerford and Savernake. The three stop signals apply to each of the platform lines. Another 'Hall' is arriving from the West Country and is signalled to the up platform, No 5, while the lowered signal is for a down West of England train. (*Les Reason*)

Left The view from Worcester Shrub Hill Junction towards the station. The Hereford line comes in from the right, and that from Birmingham on the left, with the signals 'off' for the platform. The goods lines swerve sharply around the back of the station, past the locomotive works on the far left, and on the far right of the layout is the bay platform, once frequented by 0-4-2 tanks and streamlined diesel railcars bound for Bromyard and Leominster, amongst other places. The points in the down Birmingham line in the foreground diverge to the engine shed. The up Birmingham line forks at the end of the nearest platform ramp to form the up middle line, and the same pattern was followed in the down direction, with a 'scissors' crossover being provided halfway along each platform. The layout was not a lavish one for the traffic once handled, but ample for what was running here in August 1973.

Above Looking in the opposite direction back towards Shrub Hill Junction from the down platform, with the signals cleared for the Hereford direction (left) and the Birmingham direction (right). Note the large disc hanging under the canopy, acting as a home signal. The signal box is the 1890 standard type and the passenger engine shed beyond, once packed with steam engines, now accommodates a single Class '47' diesel. Costs are being reduced, and later the carriage washing plant will go and Worcester coaches requiring servicing will be taken empty to London!

Above left On the famous 100 mph racing ground at the south end of the GWR/LNER Joint line near Northolt. Taken in very bad light, unfortunately, this shows Northolt Junction West's up relief and up main home signals and Northolt Junction East's distant signals below. From left to right the signals read: to Marylebone directing distant; Up Relief Line to Greenford; to Marylebone directing distant applying to trains turned to the Up Relief from the Up Main via the junction immediately beyond the gantry; Up Main to Up Relief Line home for West Junction; to Marylebone directing distant applying to trains on the Up Main turning off at East Junction; Up Main home for West Junction (with distant for East Junction); Down Main starter; Down Relief starter (both for West Junction). Northolt East Junction had no crossovers. At West box a 'ladder' crossover linked the four tracks. Engines returning from Kensington to the Eastern Region arrived at West box on the down side to be crossed to the up side, to take the Neasden line at East Junction. There was also a connection at West box from the Up Relief Line to South Ruislip station coal yard and the Express Dairy milk processing plant. (*Peter Barlow/Author's Collection*)

Left The St Denys gantry 2 miles north of Southampton where the Portsmouth line merged with the main line from Waterloo. The Southern Region was very fond of its old LSWR latticework 'dolls', although the gantry itself is constructed of rolled steel joists and was erected in the early 1960s replacing two separate signals, one for each route. Nonetheless, the old LSWR latticework 'dolls' make a handsome and remarkable signal, considering that all the other British Railways regions had long since abandoned, in new work, anything but tubular steel 'dolls'. The signals read, left to right: Portsmouth line to Down Local; to Down Through; to Bevois Park No 1 Reception Line; to Bevois Park No 2 Reception Line; to Down Local from Down Through; Down Through; and Bevois Park Nos 1 and 2 again.

Above I had ridden down from Oxford on this 'Merchant Navy' in 1965 and, jumping off smartly at Southampton, I took this 'snap' as much to record the fireman as anything, who is walking back to put the 'bag' (water hose) in the tender. Now the whole scene, recorded so haphazardly, is national transport history and a happy personal memory. This much-photographed gantry was at the west end of Southampton Central station and the signals read, from right to left: Down Through; Down Through to Down Local; Down Through to Goods Loop; Down Local to Down Through; Down Local; Down Local to Goods Loop; Platform line to Down Through; to Down Local; to Goods Loop.

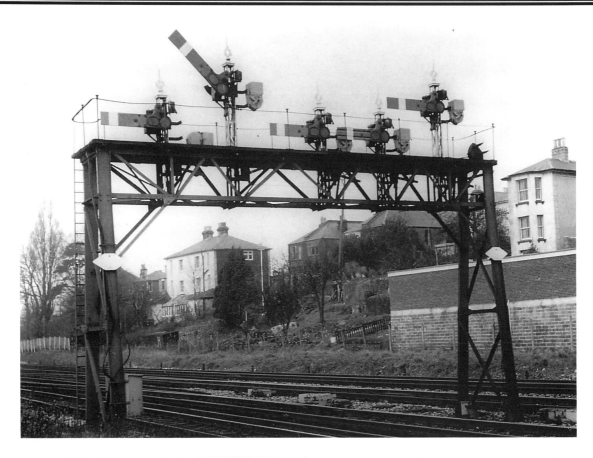

Above left The layout a short distance west from Southampton to Millbrook was quadrupled and brought into use on 2 June 1935. These are Millbrook's outer home signals in 1972, motor operated owing to their distance from the box. The signals on this gantry read, from left to right: Down Local to Docks; Down Local; Down Through to Docks; Down Through to Down Local; Down Through.

Left Southern 'King Arthur' Class No 30449 *Sir Torre* runs into or through Fleet station on the down local in 1955, its exhaust partially hiding the wooden LSWR signal box. The box and the signal gantry were brought into use on 29 September 1904, part of the Basingstoke to Woking electro-pneumatic signalling scheme covering 24 miles of quadruple track. Station areas and junctions were controlled from signal boxes as usual, but beyond 'station limits', on plain track, signals were placed at 1,500-yard intervals and were worked automatically by the passage of a train over low voltage electric circuits in the rails — 'track circuits'. These automatic lower quadrant signals normally showed 'All Right' and only rose to 'Danger' when a train had passed. When that train passed clear of the next stop signal, a track circuit was activated which caused air pressure to be fed to the power cylinder of the stop signal in the rear, which then cleared. The distant signal below it remained at 'Caution' until the train had passed beyond the second stop signal ahead. (*Peter Barlow/Author's Collection*)

Above The interior of Fleet signal box in 1955 showing a few of the 39 'draw-slide' controls — the black handles are for points and the red handles for signals. Above the handles is the instrument shelf carrying some round-cased and some rectangular-cased signal arm repeaters showing their arms at 'Danger' and 'All Right' respectively. On top of the shelf are the signalling bells by which the signalmen in the boxes on each side of Fleet — Winchfield and Farnborough — send their codes to 'ask line clear' and other signalling routines. The Fleet signalman responds to the incoming codes and transmits his own codes using the brass plungers on the front of the shelf which are labelled 'Winchfield Local', 'Winchfield Through', 'Farnborough Through', and 'Farnborough Local'. Note also the different bell shapes to produce different sounds so that the signalman will recognise which bell — out of the four — has rung.

The LSWR also used this powered signalling system at Staines, where five boxes were replaced with two in April 1904, at Clapham Junction in 1911-36, and at Salisbury. The Basingstoke–Woking installation was replaced by automatic colour-lights on 23 October 1966. (*Peter Barlow/Author's Collection*)

Above left From rural Hampshire to the smoke of the industrial North-west, and one of the biggest railway stations in Britain — Preston, Lancs. This 1952 view is looking north from a signal post near No 4 box, otherwise known as Dock Street Junction, which dated from *circa* 1904 and had a frame of 184 levers, some of which were lettered 'A' to 'P', leaving out 'I' and 'O'. Its signalmen had to be able to see into the station below Fishergate bridge so horizontal tappet interlocking was used instead of the usual vertical LNWR interlocking, which would have made the box too tall. Somewhat murkily in the distance can be seen the famous gantry of 15 posts and 35 arms which spanned the up and down through, up and down fast, and slow lines. All the stop arms on it were controlled by both No 4 box and No 5, a few hundred yards further north. The down line signals on the gantry were No 4's starters and No 5's homes, whilst the up line signals on the gantry formed No 5's starters and No 4's homes. (*Author's Collection*)

Left A wider view of Preston No 4 box in 1952, standing between the down and up fast lines. The signalmen here controlled six main 'running roads' with all the junctions between the tracks and the 'fan' of roads to serve ten passenger platform faces. They also controlled carriage sidings and a goods line on the down side, sidings on the up side and the Dock Street coal yard which could be reached from the down side by a 'ladder' crossover which spanned the entire layout — a total of 12 tracks. The end of this crossing, curving to the right into the coal yard, can be seen in the foreground. (*Author's Collection*)

Above Looking south from the No 6 Bay line at Crewe in 1940, with South signal box on the right with its 15-'doll', 45-arm gantry. These very characterful LNWR signals were operated electrically through solenoids on the signal post. (*Author's Collection*)

Above left The view in the opposite direction shows London & North Western Railway signalling in its most complicated form. The 15-'doll', 45-arm gantry at Crewe South controlled the quadruple line from Euston where the double tracks from Shrewsbury (GWR) and Alsager (North Staffs) joined and fanned out into ten through platforms, six bays, sundry goods lines and sidings. (*Author's Collection*)

Left And this is the view the Crewe South signalman would have had of his gantry — a rather splendid view, I think. Note the cylindrical solenoids on the signal posts below each arm; when energised, they forced the arm 'off'. It is said that if the signal arms remained lowered for more than 2-3 minutes, the current drawn by the solenoids caused the metal to become hot enough to fry eggs. Photographed in 1940. (*Author's Collection*)

Above The interior of Crewe South box in 1940. The frame holds 247 levers at 3½-inch centres in two tiers; the levers on the lower level stand between those on the higher level, effectively giving levers at 1¾-inch centres. The levers are interlocked via the down-rods attached to them and the tappet blades, tappets and bridle irons to which the down-rods are joined. At the lowest extremity of the tappet blades are the electrical contacts through which the circuits are made to send 110 volts at 15 amps to energise the solenoids on the signal posts. This system was designed by the LNWR's Signal Superintendent, Mr Thompson, and was built at Crewe Works and supplied with current from the LNWR's own generating station. The system was first tried in a 25-lever frame at Crewe Gresty Lane box, brought into use on 15 January 1899, this Crewe South installation being brought into use in June or July 1907. According to the *Railway Gazette*, 17 September 1920, page 350, the operating floor was gutted by a fire started by an electrical fault.

On the face of the instrument shelf there are some track circuit repeaters, the third from left showing 'Track Occupied'. On top of the shelf, nearest the camera, there are 'Train Ready to Start' indicators, labelled according to the route the train required to take. These are operated from the various platforms by the respective Platform Inspectors. Between these vital little instruments are the even more vital block telegraph instruments by which the signalmen give or refuse permission for a train to approach. The telegraph needle is switched to 'Line Clear' or 'Train on Line' by turning the circular knob at the front of the case. The Morse key by which the bell codes are sent is contained within the instrument.

One cannot help but wonder at the skill of the men who worked such places. There are at least 20 block instruments on that shelf requiring as many bells. In all the noise of heavy traffic, clanking levers, engines whistling and steam escaping, how did the signalmen keep account, in their heads, of what they were doing? And how did they hear *anything* — never mind identify exactly which bell had rung? (*Author's Collection*)

Above left 170 miles to the south, an LNWR signal box on the West London Railway, a joint GWR/LNWR company. This 1976 view is looking south from Kensington North Main towards Kensington South Main box at the other end of the station. The latter controlled North Main's distant signals in the southbound direction; the North Main signalman could pull his distant signal lever but the arm did not respond until South Main's signalman pulled *his* distant signal lever, thus releasing the 'back slot' on North Main's distants. Instead of an electric repeater inside North Main to inform the signalman when the slot had been taken off, a 12-inch diameter pivoted steel disc was fixed close to the floor inside the front wall behind North Main's distant signal lever. When South Main's distant signal wire was pulled, the movement was also used to move the pivoted steel disc which 'whacked' against a horsehair-stuffed leather cushion with a noise like a pistol shot.

Left Now looking north with North Main box in the distance, these are Kensington South Main's northbound starting signals, with North Main's distant signal, and 'Warning Acceptance' subsidiary arms at the bottom of the posts. The signals control movements along the platform or middle roads and the divergences. Note the — by 1976 — very unusual 'scissors crossover' on the right. Reversing movements over this are signalled by double GWR discs (left) and LMS discs (right).

Above An unusual juxtaposition of Southern Railway signals and a Great Western signal box at one of the several junctions between the GWR and LSWR companies. This is Salisbury, looking west from the down platform, with the GWR box beyond a fine Southern Railway bracket signal (see page 164ff). The upper arm routes from the down main towards Wilton, Yeovil Junction and the West Country, the lower to the GWR line, heading for Westbury. Note the compressed air cylinders driving the signal arms and also the elevated disc signal. The signal box was opened in 1900 and had a 95-lever frame, reduced to 65 in 1972 when this photograph was taken. It was abolished in October 1973.

Above left Another mixture. The Great Western signal box at Codford was an 1877 construction extended and rebuilt in 1895 to the standard pattern of the day. At the time of this 1973 photograph it had a 34-lever frame. The Southern 'old rails' signal, the up home, was erected after the regional boundary changes of 1950 put the ex-GWR Westbury–Salisbury branch into Southern Region ownership almost to Dilton Marsh Halt, 2 miles from Westbury.

Left The view north from Cricklewood's down fast line platform, with Cricklewood Junction's down fast line home signal and Brent Junction's distant below, and the fast to slow junction signal on the right. The signal is another example of the marriage of LNWR and MR signal construction from the immediate post-grouping period (see page 80). The left-hand 'doll' used to carry the junction signal routing left to Dudding Hill Junction and the line south to Acton. The steel signal behind and to the left carries a Dudding Hill line 'doll' on the left. This is a 'nasty', an LMR construction from the late 1960s or early '70s.

Cricklewood Junction signal box was originally called Child's Hill Junction before being renamed in 1903. It contained a Midland Railway 100-lever frame, the levers standing at 6-inch centres, which was replaced in 1944 with an LMS (REC) frame of 135 levers standing at 4½-inch centres. It was re-locked in the late 1970s to work a remodelled layout and by then had been unofficially re-named by the locking fitters as 'Moneybags Junction'. The Midland Railway wooden bracket carrying upper quadrant arms outside the box is the up local line No 2 home with a junction signal to the up fast. The box was originally all timber, but was given its protective brick skirt as an air raid precaution at the start of the Second World War.

Above Up the line towards St Pancras, St Paul's Road Passenger Junction box was opened in September 1898, replacing an earlier box, and, when photographed, it was about to be closed. It was a smoky place to work with a view of nothing but brick walls — and a constant procession of hard-working locomotives. The signal is pure Midland Railway, the design of which is believed to date from about 1880 and which continued to be manufactured with only very minor alterations until the demise of the Midland Railway in 1921.

Left In complete contrast is the box at Gort, Co Galway, in 1982, with the signalman, P. J. Cunningham, and a man who happened to be crossing the fields when he saw a conversation going on between the signalman and myself. Unable to contain his curiosity, the man changed course and climbed as far as the top of the wall where he sat for the next 2 hours. We had 'a great ould gas' and eventually the train came, very late.

Above This very humble signal box belonged to the Burry Port & Gwendraeth Valley Railway which began life in 1837 as the Kidwelly Canal & Tramroad Co and opened as a mineral railway in 1869, the rails being laid on the bed of the (drained) canal. Its purpose was to serve the many small collieries around Kidwelly. After being bankrupt from 1881 to 1898, its fortunes improved and it began carrying miners to work in coaches owned by the collieries and running a weekly shopping trip into Kidwelly for the miners' wives. This was illegal, as the railway had no licence to carry passengers, and dangerous, since the railway was in a decrepit state.

In 1903, a Board of Trade inquiry into a collision between an engine and a miners' train near Burry Port revealed the awful truth. The BP&GVR was ordered to mend its ways — literally — and that enthusiastic proponent of 'Light Railways', Colonel Stephens, was brought in to advise on how to improve the line to passenger-carrying standards as cheaply as possible. After a mere six years the BP&GVR had brought itself up to scratch and was given official permission to carry passengers.

This 'chicken-house'-style signal box is a typical example of work carried out under the direction of Colonel Stephens. Its nameboard is longer than its lever frame which consisted of only three levers, one to work the facing point and its bolt and two levers for the four signals around the junction. The signals were 'selected'; in other words the signalman pulled the 'up' direction lever or the 'down' and depending on how the points were set the required signal was lowered. The single track forked into a single line to the docks and another to the station, 418 yards from the box. The box, seen in 1956, fell into a bad state of neglect like the rest of the line, and was replaced by a brand new structure in 1959. Six years later it was closed. (*Peter Barlow/Author's Collection*)

Above left Moretonhampstead box dates from 1892 when the GWR modernised the signalling system it had inherited from the previous owners, the South Devon Railway. It first held a frame of 15 levers but this was replaced by a 12-lever frame in 1920. Originally the box had a Webb-Thompson Electric Train Staff instrument for the section through to Bovey, but at some time after 1936 this was abolished in favour of the little aluminium electric 'key token'. Signalman Davies has the token in its carrier hoop over his shoulder. The box was closed in March 1959, approximately when this photograph was taken. (*Author's Collection*)

Left Ystrad Mynach South box, perched up on the valley side, must have been a splendid place to work in steam days. Not only was it in a sylvan setting with views for miles, but it also gave the signalman a grandstand view of his quadruple track with junctions, and of the trains fairly blasting up the steep grade towards him. All this and wages too! The box was kept highly polished when I visited it in 1981 so the signalmen still appreciated what they had. It was a McKenzie & Holland signal box, built in stone for the Rhymney Railway and dating from the 1890s. In 1981 it contained a GWR lever frame of 46 levers installed in 1938.

Above Blodwell Junction, originating as part of the Tanat Valley Light Railway, which opened on 5 January 1904. The box was built by the signalling contractor, Tyers & Co of London, for the TVLR and held a Tyers frame of 20 levers. This 1954 view looks west up the Tanat valley towards Llangynog with the line to Llanymynech forking left. This branch was closed in 1925 and was lifted in 1936-8, but a short length was retained as a siding, hence the junction signalling still intact in this view; the facing point is equipped with a bolt, the Cambrian Railways junction signal still has both arms, and there is a signal to come off the branch. (*Peter Barlow/Author's Collection*)

Above left Looking north from the up platform at Barmouth, on August Bank Holiday 1974, with not a carriage or even a person in sight at what was once a very busy railway/holiday place. A GWR concrete post signal, Barmouth North box's up starter with a 'Calling on' arm below, is nearest the camera, and on the far left are several lengthy sidings, now half-hidden by grass, but which would once have been filled with the carriages of excursion trains. The signal box was built in 1890 by contractors Dutton & Co for the Cambrian Railways and was closed about 10 months after this view was taken.

Left Cwmmer Afan Junction, once the terminus of the Lynvi & Ogmore Railway (L&OR), junction for the Glyncorrwg and the Rhondda & Swansea Bay (R&SB) lines. The L&OR was absorbed into the GWR in 1883. The photograph is taken from a train about to enter a 1,591-yard-long tunnel on the way south to Maesteg and Bridgend on the ex-L&OR line. The signal box on the right is a GWR production, almost certainly dating from 1886. The GWR opened a single track extension, approximately 1¾ miles long, to a passenger station and a mine at Abergwnfi in that year and the style of the box architecture would agree with that date.

The R&SB was a double line from Aberavon (Port Talbot) docks to Cwmmer Afan, opened in 1885 and extended as a single track to Treherbert on the Taff Vale Railway at the head of the Rhondda Valley in 1890. On the left is the McKenzie & Holland box built for the R&SB and probably opened with the line in 1885. The R&SB system was worked by the GWR from 1 January 1906 and was absorbed in 1921, but the two stations and two signal boxes remained in use until 1960 when a single large signal box was installed. The R&SB ran above the GWR Abergwnfi extension for 1½ miles climbing at 1 in 45, before entering the Rhondda tunnel, 3,443 yards long, which brought the tracks out high above Treherbert.

Above Drope Junction box of 1896, avowedly a Barry Railway design but owing much to a similar design by the Great Eastern and also by Saxby & Farmer. It was built by contractors Evans O'Donnell and held a 30-lever frame. The line straight ahead is the Barry main line heading for the coal-mines high in the Valleys; the line curving round to the left behind the box is the Barry connection to the GWR main line at Peterston Junction a few miles east of Llantrisant.

Above left Matt Darcy, 45 years a railwayman, watching — with amusement and toleration — from the window of his Athlone West Junction box as I record the scene in 1982. The station stood between two junctions as the east-west Midland Great Western came from Dublin to Galway to be joined at the east end, on the far side of the Shannon bridge, by the Great Southern & Western Railway coming from Portarlington on the Dublin–Cork line. Here at the west end the MGWR forked right, north-west, for Roscommon and Sligo. Athlone West Junction box was constructed by the Railway Signal Co of Liverpool and held an RSCo frame of 61 levers plus a modern electric control console to operate the junction for the Portarlington/Mullingar junction and siding connections at the Dublin end of the station. The tall bracket signal with an elevated disc for the (ex-MGWR) engine shed is of Great Southern Railway vintage, in tubular steel; the other two signals have concrete posts.

Left This is my idea of a *really* handsome signal box — the GWR's classic standard design of 1896, built here at Cholsey & Moulsford in 1908 with very minor detail alterations. The relatively great width of these boxes is accentuated here by the apparent lack of height. The interior of this box contained a 75-lever frame and was luxuriously long and roomy and was as polished as 50-60 years of sweat, 'Brasso', elbow-grease, 'Ronuk' and stove blacking could make it. Why did signalmen, and in particular GWR men, do it? They gave up their relatively peaceful Sundays to 'bulling the place up' and for no extra pay. This remarkable example of 'Pride in the Job' was destroyed in the signalling modernization of May 1965.

The photographer was trespassing in the box on this day in 1955 when the bell of the 'Station phone' jangled out — the porter was giving a warning that 'the Guv'nor' was coming! The Cholsey Station Master was one who did not allow unauthorized persons in the signal box, so the trespasser fled precipitately to save his signalman friend embarrassment, and took up position on the down main platform — you will notice that the signal box door is still open after a very hasty exit. You might also be able to see the very stern and upright bearing of the 'SM' and also the grin and friendly wave from the porter who had sent the warning. (*Peter Barlow/Author's Collection*)

Above On a crisp, sunny day in March 1955 the Chipping Norton–Banbury train arrives, bustling into the peaceful country scene at Hook Norton. Passengers depart, doors slam, and a little girl and her grandfather stand up by the engine, admiring the fire, the fireman, the clank and clang, hiss and sing, the brightness of work-polished steel — the 'rightness' of a steam engine. At the back of his train the guard passes a few words of friendly greeting with the signalman before whistling the driver on his way. Hook Norton box was opened in 1907 and contained a frame of 33 levers. It was closed in December 1962. (*Peter Barlow/Author's Collection*)

Above left **Par station looking from the Newquay branch in 1955 with No 5500 running round its train. The signal box is of a very early type, classified 'GWR Type 2' by the Signalling Record Society. It retains its original hip roof and small-paned windows but has lost its vertical planking. When built, almost certainly in 1879, it was 17 feet 8 inches long, but was extended to 38 feet in 1893. In 1913 it received its third frame of 57 levers, which are still in use in 1990. Note the 'switch diamonds' or 'moveable elbows' in the foreground, as in the picture on pages 86-7, again clearly showing how this device gives continuous support to wheels where normally there would be a gap. It presents a 'facing point'-type situation and is usually fitted with a safety bolt. This set has no bolt because it is in a loop line not used by passenger trains. (*Peter Barlow/Author's Collection*)**

Left **This slightly 'pagoda'-shaped box is a Saxby & Farmer production for the Lancashire & Yorkshire Railway at Weeton, a few miles west of Kirkham Junction on the Preston–Blackpool line. It was opened in the 1880s and held a 10-lever frame. The situation is exceedingly awkward, being placed on a road bridge at the top of a very deep, sharply curved cutting. The immediate question which comes to a signalman-author's mind is a very practical one — how did the Weeton signalman see trains' tail-lamps on foggy days? In the down direction it would have been particularly difficult since he could not have seen the rear of the train until it had passed through the arch of the bridge and had gone well down the line, by which time it would have been almost out of sight on the bend. The line was closed to passenger traffic *circa* 1971, but the line and the signal box are still in use for freight in 1990. (*Author's Collection*)**

Above **The Furness Railway is not one which springs readily to mind in the litany of companies, but it was a very solid railway, much given to magnificent architecture, using stone, iron and glass, all of which were local industries, of exceedingly high quality and far outstripping anything produced by the 'Great' companies or the 'Premier Line'. The country stations and signal boxes had a rugged grandeur well suited to the magnificent landscape and the heavy industry the railway served. This box at Arnside once controlled the junction for the branch line north to Hincaster on the LNWR main line to Carlisle. Photographed in 1987, it must be a magnificent place to work, rising as it does from the breathtaking beauty of Morecambe Bay with the Cumbrian Hills behind and subject to all the ferocity as well as the beauty of the elements.**

Above left This very attractive style of signal box was current on the LSWR in 1884-8 and such designs were erected at stations on the then new line from Surbiton to Guildford via Cobham in 1885 and between Brockenhurst and Christchurch via Sway in 1888. Worgret Junction box, seen here in 1974, was situated about 14 miles west of Bournemouth, slightly more than a mile west of Wareham on the LSWR main line to Dorchester, and had a 16-lever Stevens frame to control the junction with the Swanage branch, the single track of which can be seen behind the box. A Tyers No 6 tablet instrument was housed in the box to control traffic over the branch. When the instrument's draw-slide was released — by an electric current sent from the other end of the section — a 'tablet' could be withdrawn. The driver carried the tablet through to the signalman at the other end of the section, who then pulled forward a handle on the side of the instrument to release his slide. The tablet was placed on the slide, the slide was pushed home and the lever pulled to raise the tablet into the stack.

Left Havenhouse box dates from the doubling of the line to Skegness and was opened in 1899 with a second-hand 22-lever frame dating from not later than 1889. The signal box design is more functional than that of Heckington but it still retains some decorative woodwork. It was constructed to the GNR pattern of the time but was built by a local firm which was allowed to include small details of its own, such as the style of barge-board. This 1984 view is looking north, towards Skegness. Note that the somersault signal arms are early LNER-pattern corrugated steel on concrete posts.

Above Heckington box, near Sleaford, was built in 1877 by the Great Northern Railway. Its interior equipment was then and for many years afterwards 'hi-tech', with its electrical apparatus and mechanical interlocking which was nothing more or less than an iron computer. Yet its exterior does not conflict with that glorious windmill — technology from the Middle Ages. The juxtaposition of the two buildings shows how modern the railway was in the late nineteenth and early twentieth century, but it also shows the dignified feelings of the technocrats of those times. When photographed in 1984 the box had an 18-lever frame installed second-hand in 1925.

Above left The designer of this Great Northern Railway gate-wheel in Thorpe Culvert signal box intended that it should last for ever. There is no suggestion here of 'built-in redundancy' or any further change beyond railways — they were here, in this form, for good. It is, perhaps, a little surprising that GNR signal boxes with very large gates, or several of them such as at Helpston, did not have a steam engine to drive the remarkably massive mechanism! Photographed in 1984.

Left The Great Northern Railway block telegraph instruments in Thorpe Culvert box in 1984. The idea originated with the 'single-needle' telegraph, used for sending telegrams, and indeed these instruments could be used to send the visual Morse code used in that system. The beautifully shaped mahogany handle is fixed to its spindle by a massive brass clamp, and by moving the handle to the left the signalman causes the needle to deflect to the right into the 'Line Clear' sector.

The difference between this telegraph instrument and one for sending ordinary messages is that the handle remains where it is placed rather than springing back to the vertical position. It is then said to be 'blocked' left or right, hence the term 'block telegraph' which controls access to the 'block sections' between signal boxes. A signalman always *gives* permission for a train to approach from the box 'in rear', and *asks* permission to send it on to the box 'in advance'. This sometimes confuses lay persons. The situation at Thorpe Culvert is that Wainfleet is the box 'in rear' on the up line but is the box 'in advance' on the down line. Little Steeping is the box 'in advance' on the up line and the box 'in rear' on the down line.

A block section must only be occupied by one train at a time. The tall instrument with the handle, marked 'From Wainfleet', is used by the Thorpe Culvert signalman to give 'Line Clear' permission for a train to enter the block section between Wainfleet and Thorpe Culvert. When that train passes Wainfleet, the signalman there sends 'Train entering Section' — 2 beats on the bell — which the Thorpe Culvert man acknowledges by repetition and by switching the handle of his instrument to move the needle to the 'Train on Line' position. There it stays until the train, complete with its tail-lamp, has passed 440 yards ahead of Thorpe Culvert's up home signal. The signalman then sends 2-1 — 'Train out of Section' — on the Morse key projecting from the front of the small wooden box between the instruments and places the block telegraph instrument's handle centrally once more, at the 'Line Blocked' position, ready for the routine to begin again. The instrument nearest the camera is the block instrument for the section 'in advance' on the down main and is operated by the Wainfleet signalman by means of the handle on his block telegraph instrument. The far instruments work to and from Little Steeping box. The large box with the brass knob in the centre of the shelf is the 'Block Switch' by means of which Thorpe Culvert is switched into or out of the circuit of block telegraph wires. Here it is 'switched in'.

Above Saxmundham box, seen here in 1983, appears to be built to the standard Great Eastern design of 1877-8 although this particular box had a brick base to accommodate the locking room and was opened *circa* 1882. It had oversailing eaves which helped to shade the box interior; the barge-boards on GER boxes varied from plain boards to great elaboration depending, one supposes, on the whim of the contractors who built them. Saxmundham's barge-boards have some very token notches, hardly worth troubling with. Halesworth, the next box north, had plain boards.

Above left Great Eastern Railway block telegraph instruments at Saxmundham. The white plunger gives 'Line Clear' to the box in rear, Melton, and when Melton sends '2 beats' the signalman turns the flap to cover the white plunger and uncover the red one, as here, which he then pushes to bring the block telegraph needle to 'Train on Line'. The single knob on the small box below the block instrument is a plunger to send bell signals back to Melton.

Left Tunbridge Wells West B box (renamed No 2 box in 1957) was a Saxby & Farmer box with a Saxby 29/30-lever frame opened either in 1866-7 around the time of the opening of the line or in 1888 when the station was re-signalled. The single track in the foreground to Grove Junction on the Victoria–Eastbourne main line was operated by the Train Staff and Ticket system assisted by block telegraph. (*Dr Ian Scrimgeour/Courtesy Signalling Record Society*)

Above The interior of the box looking along the single track to Grove Junction, showing the very uncomfortable-looking floor-plates of the frame and the ancient Walker's instrument at the far end of the shelf. Grove Junction gave this box 'Line Clear' on the Walker's instrument, and to enable Tunbridge Wells West No 2 to give 'Line Clear' *to* Grove Junction there was on the shelf a small box-like instrument carrying a pair of plungers, one white ('Line Clear') and one red ('Train on Line'). (*Dr Ian Scrimgeour/Courtesy Signalling Record Society*)

Above The interior of Tunbridge Wells West No 2 looking towards the station. There were three tracks through the station to No 1 box, each having a separate instrument by the signalling contractor Tyer, more or less standard equipment on the LB&SCR. (*Dr Ian Scrimgeour/Courtesy Signalling Record Society*)

Above right This rather splendid little box controlled the level crossing and goods yard terminus of the 'goods only' branch from the LB&SCR at New Cross to Deptford Wharf on the south bank of the Thames. It was opened in 1904 and appears to have been constructed to an LB&SCR design dating from 1898. It held a 12-lever frame. Note the bell on the outside wall on which the signalman gave warning of the approach of a train to shunters and others at work on the line. Photographed *circa* 1951. (*Author's Collection*)

Right Tisbury station in 1957; the cameraman is standing in the down main line, looking towards Salisbury on the ex-LSWR main line from Waterloo to Exeter. The signal box is the LSWR's 'Mark 1' design, cramped, dark, cheap and, dare I say it, ugly. Inside the box one entered a room over-crammed merely — at first glance — with the usual steel, brass and mahogany equipment, highly polished from years of wear. On looking closer, perhaps when one's eyes become used to the twilight, the magnificent eccentricity of the equipment became apparent . . . (*Dr Ian Scrimgeour/Courtesy Signalling Record Society*)

Above Tisbury signal box interior, looking east, in 1957. On top of the shelf the block instruments are the 'standard' LSWR Preece 'two-position' types. With the miniature signal arm in the 'Danger' position the instrument is misleading the signalman by not informing him whether the section to the rear is occupied by a train or empty — the instrument's indication is the same in either case. In this situation the signalman would be well advised to keep a precise account in his train register of the passing times of trains.

On the front face of the shelf there are some small brass-cased signal arm and track circuit repeaters. The plunger to the left of 'No 12' signal repeater (the up main distant) operates the block bell to Semley, the next block post westwards. The bell plunger to Chilmark, the next box eastwards, is next to signal repeater '2' (the down main home). The lever frame is the usual Stevens production for the LSWR, numbered 1-12, but, with eight 'Russell' levers in addition, it actually contains 20.

Mr Russell, Signal Superintendent of the Exeter Division of the LSWR, patented an inappropriately named 'lever-saving applicance' in 1892 which was intended for use at crossover roads where one point lever and two ground signal levers were required. In fact, Russell's patent device saved no levers but it did save space and did away with the need for the usual interlocking between signal and point levers.

The Stevens point lever and its two 'Russell' ground signal levers came through the same slot in the floor-plate. The point lever (a) stood in front of the ground signal levers (e) and (f) which had to be cranked left and right of the point lever so as to make their handles accessible to the signalman. It is obvious that neither (e) nor (f) could be pulled over until (a) had been reversed.

In the photograph, the straight Stevens lever 6, 'Up Sidings Points', has been pulled right across to the far left and the 'Russell' lever '6a', 'Main to Siding Disc', is slightly more than half way across the frame, the full extent of the pull necessary to bring the disc 'off'. 'Russell' lever 6b would operate the ground signal from the siding to the main line — it was up to the signalman to select the correct lever.

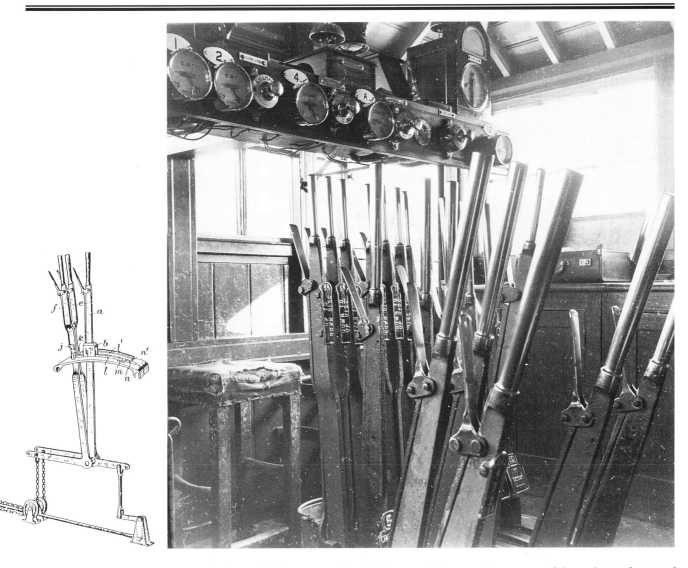

The frame was very untidy to look at with levers standing in four positions — when some of the point and ground signal levers were reversed — and with the pulling handles and latch handles of the 'Russell' signal levers shorter and higher up the lever to keep them clear of the Stevens point levers in the cramped layout.

The Stevens signal levers carried a brass at the top giving instructions as to what levers to pull in order to release the interlocking on that particular lever. For example, lever 12 top brass states 'Pull 9 10 11 for', and at the foot of the lever is a second brass reading '12 Up Distant'. Stevens point levers carried one brass at the foot, a typical legend being, as here, '7 Cross Over Road Points West'. The 'Russell' ground signal levers behind and to each side of No 7 each had a brass on which the letters were cast vertically below the number which was horizontal, viz '7a Up to Down Disc'.

Above Tisbury signal box interior looking west. The down line signal levers, 4, 3, 2 and 1, the latter being the down distant, have been reversed — perhaps for a 'Merchant Navy' Class locomotive on the 'Atlantic Coast Express' — and the circular brass-cased signal arm repeaters in the top left-hand corner — 1, 2 and 4 — are showing 'off'. There is no repeater for No 3, the down starter, because that is well in sight of the signalman. Track circuit repeater 'A' is showing 'Occupied', so the down train is not far from the signal box. The miniature signal arm in the Preece's block instrument at the right-hand end of the shelf is lowered showing that Semley has given 'Line Clear' to Tisbury for a down train to approach. Note the wonderfully battered, horsehair-stuffed, Dickensian stool, probably as old as the signal box. The attaché-case on the locker suggests that a relief signalman is working the box. This was certainly what many of the travelling signalmen used to carry their sandwiches, rule books, extra train notices and other on-duty oddments. This working museum of delights was destroyed on 12 October 1957 when a new box and frame was installed. (*Dr Ian Scrimgeour/Courtesy Signalling Record Society*)

Above left I feel closer in spirit to the people in this picture, taken *circa* 1921, and the spirit of public service in which they believed, than to the spirit — if any spirit there be — of British Rail in the late twentieth century. From left to right, back row, we see Signalmen Alf Joyce and Walt Norton, and Porters Jack Grace and Ern Essex. Left to right in the front row sit Booking Clerk Miss Hancock, Station Master Mr Hancock, and Signalman Walt Thomas.

Alf Joyce was born in 1880 and came to the GWR in July 1899 as a Lad Porter at Highclere. He then worked Lavington box, on the GWR's 'Stert cut-off', from the moment of its opening to goods traffic in July 1900 (passenger trains were allowed over the line from October of that year). He was later promoted to Wantage Road and was the first signalman in the new box at Yarnton Junction which was equipped with a frame of miniature levers working the points and signals electrically. Two months later he was demoted by 1 shilling a week to Bedwyn, and in September 1910 he came to Uffington box, retiring from the same signal box in 1945.

Walt Thomas was born in 1885 and started on the GWR as a 'Cart boy' at Paddington in June 1902. After several moves around the London Division he went to Shrivenham in 1908, but moved to Uffington in February 1914. He and Alf Joyce clubbed together to buy a piece of land from the Craven estate in Uffington village and on it they built a substantial semi-detached house which is still lived in by their descendants. Walt retired from Uffington in 1951. (*Courtesy Bill Mattingley*)

Left The inheritors of that GWR spirit of 'Pride in the Job' and 'Public Service', Jim Spinage (left) and Elwyn Richards in Uffington box in 1966. Elwyn joined the GWR from South Wales in 1930 — his first posting was Sparkford — and he worked with Walt Thomas and Alf Joyce from 1942 onwards. Jim came to the Western Region in about 1950 and I was happy and privileged to work with them both from 1960 until 1968, when Uffington box was destroyed.

Above One of the best raconteurs I met in a job full of raconteurs was Tom Baber of Frome North box, pictured in 1973, the inevitable 'Gold Flake' roll-up in his fingers and in the middle of some fascinating account of his early life in Dorset, or his father's attempt to make his fortune in the steel mills of Pittsburgh at the turn of the century. He had a gravelly, cider-soaked voice and spoke the 'Darset' accent beautifully. He was also a champion Victoria sponge-cake maker. Note the toasting fork, teapot, battered armchair and dining table.

Above far left During the two great wars the railway system was of vital importance to the war effort — Winston Churchill stated as much in 1945. Without the railwaymen and women — and the wives who stayed at home to wash and cook for their menfolk — the railway would have ceased to run and military equipment would not have been moved. All this was down to such men as Tom Baber and Tudor Rees, seen here going home on his 'auto-cycle' from the temporary Savernake Tunnel West box in 1944. (*Courtesy Doreen Stevens, who as Doreen Spackman was signalwoman at Collingbourne Ducis, M&SW section, GWR*)

Above left Signalman George Young, looking rather formidable in Swindon Locomotive Yard box in 1961.

Left Signalman Bill (Doctor) Curtis who came to Knighton Crossing from the Midland & South Western Junction Railway at the grouping in June 1923. Bill seriously damaged his ankle at Weyhill in 1915 (see my *Signalman's Twilight*) hence his awkward stance here. I was privileged to work with and get to know Bill, and at the age of 83 he was still doing voluntary work for the Red Cross, receiving the BEM in recognition. (*Courtesy Bill Curtis*)

Above Signalman P.J. Cunningham in Gort box in 1982 (see page 104). He has withdrawn the miniature electric train staff for the section to Ennis and has it in the pick-up hoop ready to hand to the driver of the train.

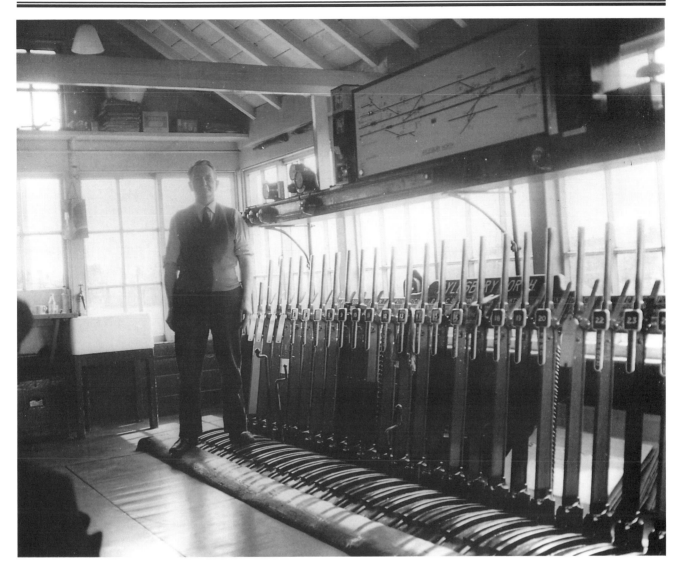

Left Signalman Larry Glynn in Dublin Harcourt Street box, ex-Dublin & South Eastern Railway. His hand is resting on a lever of the electric frame designed and built by the Great Southern Railway of Ireland and first installed at Pearse Station (Westland Row) in the centre of Dublin in 1935. There are two electric power frames of six levers separated by a conventional mechanical frame of seven levers; the small levers operate the station's colour-light signals and the large levers work the points. All 19 levers are interlocked by a conventional, horizontal tappet machine with additional electric locks operated by track circuits. The block telegraph instrument is by Harper, an apt name for the signalling instrument widely used on Irish double track railways. Larry Glynn became signalman at Liffey Junction, on the opposite side of the city, when Harcourt Street closed in December 1958. (*Peter Barlow/Author's Collection*)

Above Aylesbury North box in 1961 with its Railway Signal Company frame, standard equipment on the Great Central's London Extension. The almost invisible block instrument in a black and white metal box at the far end of the track diagram is, of course, of British Railways origin. This was the first box I photographed off the Western Region and its signalman was delighted to show me round.

Above left Leicester North box, Midland Railway, was opened in May 1911, a handsome piece of industrial architecture overshadowed in 1975 by late twentieth century barbarity. The BR(LMR) signals direct up main line trains to Platform 3 (right-hand arm), Platform 2 and the up goods line. Below are Leicester London Road box's distant signals. The single-'doll' bracket signal on the left is on the up goods line. It was extremely rare to see the distant signals raised so, one week before closure, an enthusiastic railwayman asked the London Road signalman to pull the up main distant for the one non-stop train of the day. He obliged and the driver of the train was so surprised that he stopped at London Road signal box and queried the correctness of the signal!

Left The signalman in Leicester North box was busy sorting out traffic problems on a very hot day when I called. The 65-lever frame is an LMS tappet-locked type dating from 1943, installed here during the 1950s. Notice the miserable British Railways block instruments on the shelf and the LMS lever frame with *plastic*-covered lever handles — yuk! Note too, by the window on the right, a splendid wooden armchair doubtless of Midland Railway origin. The signal box and its 65-lever frame were abolished in June 1986 under a signalling automation plan.

Above The Leicester North box diagram showing the tracks controlled. At the left-hand end of the diagram, the bottom line is a siding, then in order the lines are Down Main, Up Main, Down Goods, Up Goods, Up Siding.

Above left Broad Street box (originally designated 'Broad Street No 2') was an 1880s production of the North London Railway's signal works at Bow. After the passage of 100 years — and a great deal of hostile attention from the Luftwaffe in 1940-3 (note the brick wall in front of the original wall as a protection against bomb blast) — it is still a handsome building with a touch of the Italianate in its timber upperworks. Photographed in 1975.

Left The 73 levers and floor-plate of the frame in Broad Street box were by Stevens, but the interlocking beneath the floor was renewed in 1971-2 using Railway Signal Co locking boxes brought second-hand from Colwich North box, Nottingham. This re-locking was due to the abolition of Broad Street No 1 box (North London Railway tappet locking, *circa* 80 levers), Skinner Street (North London Railway tumbler locking, *circa* 65 levers) and New Inn Yard (NLR tappet, *circa* 70 levers).

Above The curiously named North Pole Junction — was there once a pub nearby called 'The North Pole'? — was the parting of the ways for the LNWR and GWR on their joint line from Kensington. The LNWR signal box, seen here in 1976, had a frame of 30 levers to control the junction, the LNWR continuing steeply uphill and over the GWR main line by a bridge towards Willesden, whilst the GWR dropped down to the right then swung sharply left, westwards, through the embankment to join the main line at Old Oak Common. On 1 April 1863 a double line was laid from the main line at West London Junction (Ladbroke Grove) to North Pole Junction. By this route GWR passenger trains had worked from Paddington to Victoria — and even to Brighton. In the 1930s it was used for non-passenger workings into West London Carriage Sidings when there was no block telegraph between Ladbroke Grove and North Pole Junctions.

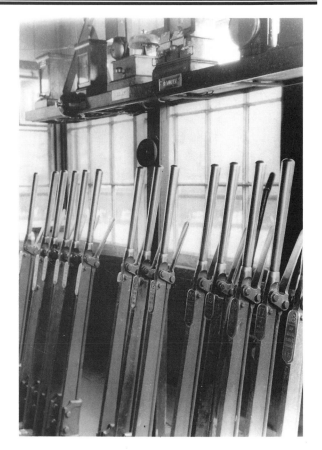

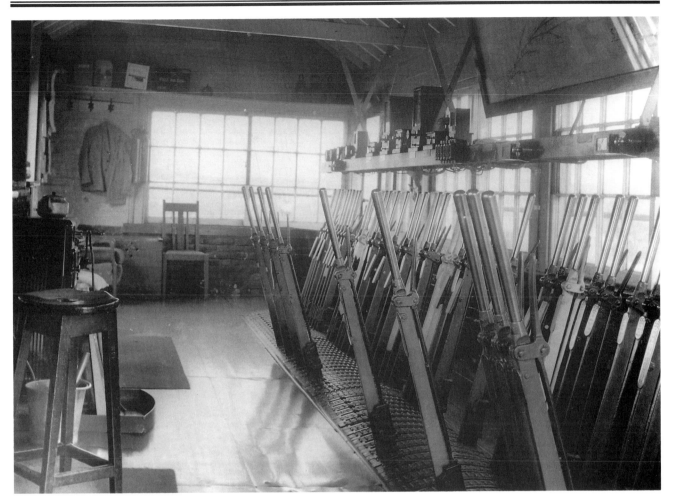

Above far left The LNWR levers in North Pole Junction, immensely robust and, not to put too fine a point on it, highly individualistic. I arrived here on foot at 9 am one Sunday morning to find a West Indian signalman in charge who shared his breakfast with me. He spoke of his enjoyment of railway work and his appreciation of all those lovely 'priv' tickets which enabled him to visit the length and breadth of England with his family. My kind of railwayman.

Above left The interior of Abingdon box with its 18 exceptionally neat and polished GWR levers. The date of opening of the box is not yet known but the box architecture suggests about 1883. The 2½-mile single track to the main line at Radley was worked by the wooden Train Staff and Ticket system, the routine of signalling being carried out on the block instruments on the shelf. (*Peter Barlow/Author's Collection*)

Left A winter teatime shunting session at Abingdon in 1954 as the engine stables its 70-foot auto-coach. The Abingdon branch was, like that to Calne, a prosperous branch serving a bustling town with plenty of vigorous industry. On the extreme right, the deep shadow is cast by a long row of covered vans, probably waiting to deliver parts to the MG car factory. (*Peter Barlow/Author's Collection*)

Above St Erth signal box, opened in 1899, had a 69-lever frame to control the station, sidings, junction and single track 4¼-mile branch to St Ives. The signals have been lowered for the departure of an up train — levers 61, 62 and 63 (bay line starter to branch, branch starter and branch advanced starter) are reversed in the foreground. The next lever which is reversed in No 53, the bolt for the 'Up Main to Down Branch' facing points. Note the high polish, the tall GWR-issue stool for use at the booking desk, the big black enamelled stove with its teapot and coal bucket, and the domestic chairs.

The Great Western rebuilt Birmingham Snow Hill station in 1910-13 without interrupting the traffic. The station and tracks were on arches and space was very limited so it was an obvious place to install a compact all-electric lever frame which did not require wide 'runs' of point rodding or dozens of signal wires on their pulleys, and which could be raised above the tracks. The GWR had been experimenting with electric frames by McKenzie & Holland at Didcot North Junction (1905) and Yarnton Junction (1909) but the Birmingham frames were by Seimens, brought into use at Birmingham North and Hockley in 1910 and at Birmingham South in 1913.

This is Birmingham North in 1957 with 224 levers at 2½-inch centres. On the shelf is a Tyers signal arm repeater for signal 109, the No 12 platform down starter, and next to that is a Tyers 'Train Describer' which indicates to the signalman the destination of an approaching train. Next to that again is the 'non-pegging' part of the unique block instruments designed for the North and South boxes. On this instrument, South box gives 'Line Clear' and 'Train on Line' to North box, and these indications appear within the large white area. Below that are six small apertures and these are used to keep count of the number of trains or light engines occupying that particular line between the North and the South boxes, for all platform lines except Nos 1 and 2 are worked on the 'Permissive' principle. As each successive train occupies the platform line to which this instrument applies, the relevant number appears in successive apertures. When six trains or engines are present, the instrument will read 'Blocked Back'. (*Peter Barlow/Author's Collection*)

Birmingham North power frame, showing most of the 224 levers. On 28 October 1940 Birmingham was bombed and the battery house at Snow Hill was destroyed. On 8 November power had been restored to the point motors but signalling was still by hand flag. At 7.20 pm that day the air raid sirens wailed again and the signalmen continued to work in almost total darkness — just a couple of blue light bulbs. The 1.45 pm Paddington was ready to leave through points 176. Looking at the close-spaced ranks of levers — they are placed at 2½-inch centres, and the designers had never considered the possibility of aerial bombardment and 'black-out precautions' — it is easy to see how the signalman pulled over 173 in the darkness. He then went to the window and told his handsignalman to let the train go. The driver was anxious to leave Birmingham, so started with great vigour and in the darkness did not see that he was running up the engine spur where he collided with No 2249, hitting it clean over the buffer stops and demolishing a large bracket signal. Such were the difficulties of railwaymen long ago. By the bye, No 2249 was several times the victim of such assaults, being 'hit off the road' at Honeybourne and Hinksey Yard during the war.

Nearest to the camera is the 'box to box' telephone and just beyond that is a 'pegging' block instrument with a plunger to send 'Line Clear' back to South box and a knob which is turned to register each additional train or engine which occupies the platform after the first. (*Peter Barlow/Author's Collection*)

Above left The LMS(REC) frame numbered 1-50 in Tebay box in 1966 with a nice pair of LNWR block instruments on the shelf. The LMR installed the frame in December 1952, Midland Railway fashion, that is against the back wall, leaving the windows clear of instruments. Another MR technique used here is that levers working siding points, crossovers and their associated signals occupy the extremities of the frame with the important main and branch line signal levers at the centre of the row, supposedly conveniently placed close to the signalling instruments. The reversed lever nearest to the camera, No 27, is the blue facing point bolt lever for the 'Down Main to Branch' facers. Reversed next to that is red lever No 32, the up main starter, with its white 'Released by Line Clear' band. Next again is No 35, red top, yellow bottom, and 'Line Clear Release' band, which operates the down intermediate block signal between Tebay and Scout Green. Tebay's down main starter, No 36, is reversed alongside.

Left 'Getting the road' from Gobowen North, the signalman in Weston Rhyn box taps out '4 beats' on the Morse key of a GWR block bell, 'Is Line Clear for an Express Train?'. The reply will ring out a high-pitched 'ting' on the 'church dome' bell. Behind the signalman is the gate-wheel with the rack which it drives to operate the gates. Photographed in 1977. (*John Morris*)

Above The instruments in Weston Rhyn box are a very early GWR/Spagnoletti pattern. C.E. Spagnoletti, the GWR's Telegraph Superintendent from 1855, designed the instrument in 1863 and it was standard equipment on the Metropolitan Railway, both overground and underground, from that date and also on the GWR, in this form or a later, more compact edition. The left-hand instrument is keyless and is operated from Gobowen North box, the 'box in advance' on the up line. Next comes the 'block bell' and then the keyed instrument, operated by the Weston Rhyn signalman to give 'Line Clear' to (or take 'Train on line' from) Gobowen North box — the 'box in rear' on the down line. Next to this is the keyed instrument working with Ruabon, the next box north. Notice how the up line instruments have white faces and the down line instruments green faces. Hanging on the shelf is a circular lever collar which would be dropped over a lever handle as a reminder not to pull that lever. (*John Morris*)

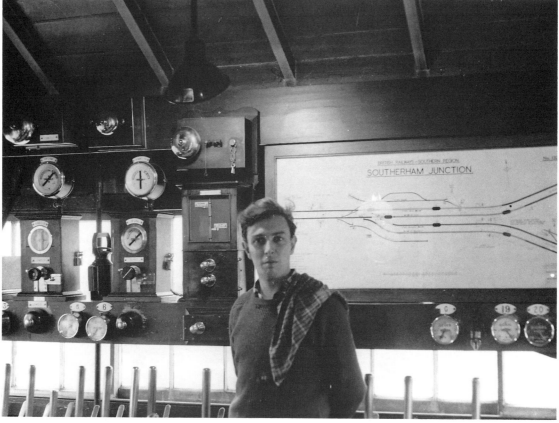

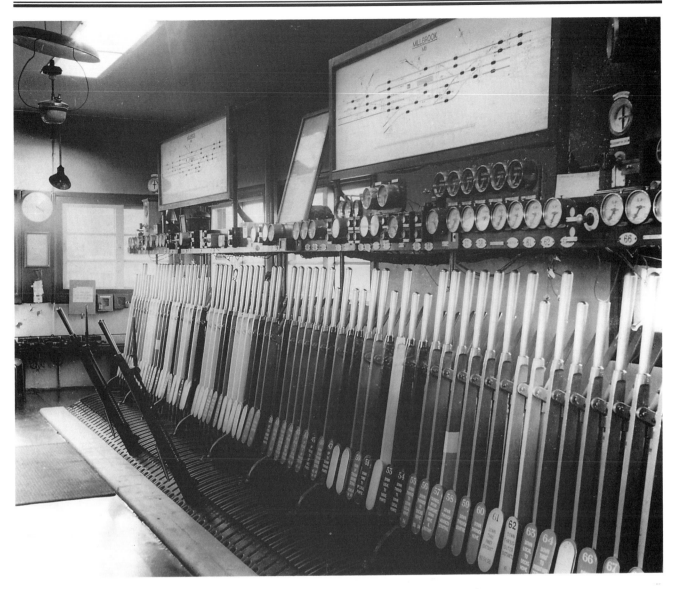

Above left A Lancashire & Yorkshire Railway interior at Thornton Station in the Fylde in 1960. Here the keyed and keyless instruments have been placed in one cabinet, as was generally the case on most railways once the waste of having separate cabinets was realised. The lower dial works to the box 'in rear', the upper dial to the box 'in advance'. The berth track circuit repeater, indicating the presence of a train outside the home signal, is screwed to the side of the block instrument, an excellent idea which the GWR did not adopt. The box housed a 20-lever frame dating from the 1880s. (*Author's Collection*)

Left A mixture of LB&SCR, Southern Railway and Southern Region equipment in 23-lever Southerham Junction, *circa* 1957. I wish I knew the signalman's name — note the famous duster over his shoulder. The left-hand block instruments are by Tyer & Co for the Southern Railway — that on the far left works with Lewes, the other with Glynde towards Eastbourne. The third is a Tyers instrument dating from LB&SCR days and works with Southease on the Newhaven branch (the lowest pair of lines of the Southern Region diagram). On the SR instruments, the wooden cabinets with the black knobs are the instruments on which 'Line Clear' is given to the box 'in rear', the block indicators for the section ahead being the circular instruments above. Above these, the bells for the instruments are close to the rafters. (*W. L. Kenning*)

Above Millbrook box dates from the Southampton–Millbrook quadrupling of 1935. The frame is a 70-lever Westinghouse 'A2' pattern, widely used by the SR at this time. I tried a few levers and found that they pulled very much more smoothly and easily than anything I had come across on my ex-GWR frames at home. The signalman was, as you can see, lavishly equipped with indicators and repeaters for signal arms, lamps and track circuits.

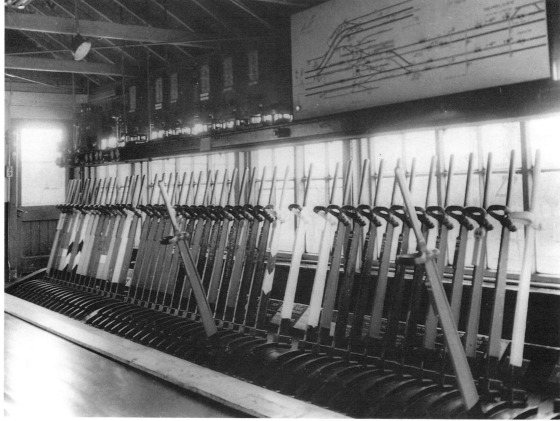

Above left Millbrook was a very busy place indeed; the signal arms really did 'go up and down like yo-yos' and one had to be very quick and alert to operate the train service successfully. It was a good job that the 'A2' frame was so easy to pull. The Millbrook signalman controlled the line to Southampton docks (at the bottom of the diagram) and four running lines east; he also had the additional problem of 'margining' trains from the down local to the down main and from the up main to the up local where the quadruple tracks merged into an ordinary double line (at the left-hand end of the diagram). And then there were Tanner's Brook down intermediate signals to be remembered and operated through lever 57. On top of all this there was traffic in and out of the freightliner terminal (at the top of the diagram) and the shunting associated with that. The brass-cased signal arm repeaters are largely of Southern Railway vintage, and 57, 58 and 59 show 'off'. Photographed in 1973.

Left Leighton Buzzard No 1 box was the first LNWR box I ever saw. It was a considerable shock. The difference between North Western and Great Western equipment and the atmosphere the equipment created was very great. Those massive, clumsy-looking levers, numbered 1-68, and the huge old LNWR block instruments, the gloomy, cavernous interior (the box had an important regulatory function and had extra space for a traffic controller's office), the use of cast-iron lever function plates on a board behind the levers instead of brass lever badges — indeed, the almost total lack of brass — created a very strong, peculiarly LNWR atmosphere. It must also be said that the LNWR equipment, crude though it looked to GWR eyes, was ruggedly hard-wearing. Crewe-built interlocking would last for twice the time of interlocking built at Reading — *pax* all you GWR fanatics, for I am quoting from real life and from an experienced Western Region signal engineer! Photographed in 1961.

Above Southcote Junction box, 2½ miles south-west of Reading station on the 'Berks & Hants' line, was opened in about 1896. At the date of this picture, 1960, it had a lever frame numbered 1-34, although originally it was numbered to 35. The original frame had about seven fewer levers but several alterations took place over the years, not least being the construction of the Coley branch to Reading Central Goods depot, running behind the box. The signal box was closed under the Reading automated signalling scheme on 25 April 1965. (*Author's Collection*)

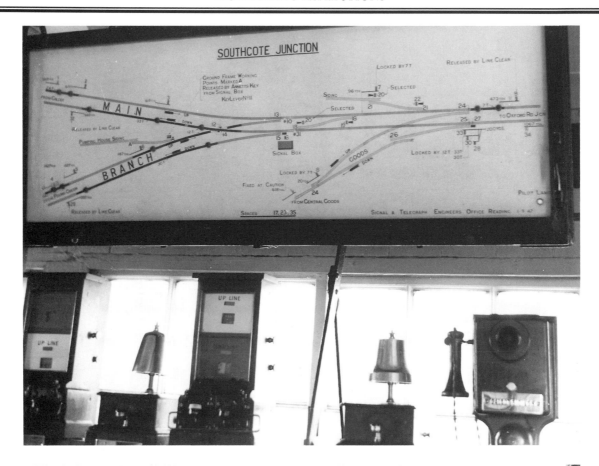

Above left The box diagram, drawn in September 1947 and photographed in 1955, shows the 'goods only' Coley branch, opened in May 1908, turning off the B&H line at points 25; the single track was worked with a wooden Train Staff. The signal box is marked by the rectangle below the down B&H line, but is wrongly sited adjacent to the left-hand divergence of the GWR branch line to Basingstoke and the GWR B&H Line to Newbury. The junction points, No 15, lay normally for the Newbury direction. Note the stylized method of indicating on the diagram the 'switch diamonds' or the 'moveable diamonds' (called 'elbows' by railwaymen) and their bolts where the up branch crosses the down main to trailing point 13; these were worked by levers 12 and 14. The siding in the 'V' of the main junction served a water pumping station. Note the ancient telephone and the GWR block bells and instruments. (*Peter Barlow/Author's Collection*)

Left An everyday — almost an every ten minutes — sight for the Southcote Junction signalman. No 4930 *Hagley Hall* (now preserved on the Severn Valley Railway) is about to pass the box on a down 'B' headcode passenger train, probably for the Newbury direction, in 1955. The Coley branch can be seen running out of view on the right. (*Peter Barlow/Author's Collection*)

Above Great Western 1880s opulence in Sarnau box, west of Carmarthen, in 1980. The ornate cast-iron bracket with the 'foliage' motif was also seen in smaller sizes. Foliage was 'all the rage' at that time, for a similar idea was used in the signal box lamp wall bracket, which was sometimes made in black-painted copper and was rewarding to polish. Note the Tilley paraffin pressure lamp hanging from the bracket; the fuel was contained in the circular tank, and the air was compressed with a bicycle pump through the connection seen on the left.

Above left Opened in about 1885, in 1980 Sarnau had GWR 1947-pattern block instruments and bells. Their brass labels are, however, almost certainly as old as the box. The box had a frame numbered to 14 which was removed for preservation after an automation scheme in March 1979.

Left Sarnau level crossing gate wheel. Note the massive ratchet in the tall rack; the signalman eased the wheel to take the pressure off the rack and release the ratchet, then pulled the ratchet handle, dropping it through 180 degrees. He could then turn the wheel to work the gates. The ratchet clanked noisily and rhythmically — an unforgettable noise — followed by the 'thud-crash' of the big gates coming against the iron stops on the gate posts. Note also the curious 'treads' between the levers. This was a short-lived and, as far as I can tell, quite useless GWR idea. I suppose the intention was to give the signalman's foot a place to rest while he pulled the lever, but the man who thought of it had obviously never pulled a lever. In practice, one's right foot rested on the tread at the linoleum end and one leaned forward from that position to pull.

Above The Stratford on Avon & Midland Junction Railway, the 'SMJ' or 'Slow, Moulding & Jolting', was a shareholder's nightmare and a railway enthusiast's dream. It was a poverty-stricken, straggling, gloriously meandering single track from east to west across the heart of the English shires, a working museum from Broom Junction, north of Evesham, to Blisworth on the West Coast Main Line and thence to Ravenstone Wood Junction south of Northampton on the MR's branch to Bedford. It was built in stages by a variety of companies and Fenny Compton (East & West Junction Railway) was opened in 1871. The E&WJR tracks ran in from the west and turned south through their Fenny Compton station which lay right alongside the existing GWR station; they then ran southwards alongside the GWR for 1½ miles before climbing and turning east, crossing the GWR by a bridge.

Each company maintained a signal box at Fenny Compton, close enough for the signalmen to talk to each other, but in May 1931 the direst financial straits persuaded the GWR and LMS to forget old hostilities and share a single signal box which was built on the site of the old GWR box. My picture is of the 1931 signal box, an LMS design showing an exactly 50/50 mixture of LNWR and MR design — LNWR to floor, MR to roof — demonstrating that whilst the LMS and the GWR might have sunk their differences, the sheer hatred between ex-LNWR and ex-MR signalling designers dating from the Grouping ten years earlier had in no way abated. Photographed in 1955. (*Peter Barlow/ Author's Collection*)

Above left Fenny Compton box housed two lever frames, one for each side of the layout. This is the LMS frame for the SMJ side — the GWR frame is behind the camera, on the left-hand side of the box. Through the doorway, signal 28, the WR down main home, can be faintly seen. The booking desk and lockers are on the left, and to the right of the door are a pair of Webb-Thompson electric train staffs for the block sections from Burton Dassett to Fenny Compton and Fenny Compton to Byfield. On the far right is a miniature electric train staff instrument for the 'long section' — Fenny Compton to Woodford West — when Byfield was switched out. Note also the 'Tilley' hanging from the roof. In March 1960, a new 65-lever frame, numbered 1-77, was opened to control an improved layout. (*Peter Barlow/Author's Collection*)

Left The SMJ was a 'goods only' line from 5 April 1952 but was used quite well. After March 1960 it became a major route for iron ore trains from the Wellingborough area to South Wales hauled by '9F' Class 2-10-0s. This view of *circa* 1954, looking towards Stratford on Avon, shows lonely Clifford Sidings box, erected here second-hand from an unknown location in September 1942 when the route from here to Stratford, seven-eighths of a mile, was doubled. Once the passenger service was withdrawn the double track was worked 'permissively' — more than one train was permitted to occupy the section at any one time. In this picture the driver is about to hand to the Clifford Sidings signalman the large Webb-Thompson electric train staff for the section from Ettington, or the previous box eastwards if Ettington was switched out. The curious thing about this view is that the engine is running on the wrong track. (*Peter Barlow/Author's Collection*)

Above Summer sunshine streaming through the Railway Signal Company levers in Ballingrane Junction box, Co Limerick, in 1975. The line from Limerick to here was opened in 1856 and extended to Foynes village and harbour in 1858. The divergence of the 'North Kerry' line from Ballingrane went down through the hills to Newcastle West in 1867 and on through the hills to Listowel and Tralee in December 1880.

Above left A closer view of the electric staff instruments in Ballingrane Junction in 1975. Nearest is the LNWR/Webb-Thompson 'large staff' for the 'North Kerry' line to Rathkeale, while the other is the Railway Signal Co's miniature staff for Foynes. The Foynes line was still in use for an occasional freight train but the 'North Kerry' line had seen no traffic — except the annual weed-killing train — since 1 January 1963.

Left No photograph can do justice to Shrewsbury Severn Bridge signal box. It is enormous, cliff-like, towering so high above a maze of tracks because the bulky LNWR interlocking machinery was housed on two floors below the levers. It was part of the LNWR/GWR Joint Station and was opened in June 1903 with, at that time, 144 working levers. Photographed in 1977.

Above The interior of Shrewsbury Severn Bridge box, showing less than half the frame. On the shelf are GWR 1947-pattern block instruments with Fletcher's-pattern train describers. The booking desk is at the far end. Once an incredibly busy place with a booking lad and an Inspector acting as 'traffic regulator', the signal box in 1977 was a shadow of its former self, handling a very much reduced service — hence the relaxed position of the signalman in the foreground.

Above left Over Junction, about 1½ miles west of Gloucester, in 1955. In the foreground is the route to South Wales via Grange Court, Chepstow and Severn Tunnel Junction. This section, from Gloucester to Chepstow (East), was opened in September 1851, the route from Chepstow (West) to Swansea having already opened in June 1850. Brunel completed one span on his bridge over the Wye at Chepstow, permitting single-line working across the river, in July 1852, thus completing through rail communication from Paddington to Swansea. Over Junction was created on 20 March 1854 when the Docks branch was opened from here. The track forking right in this view is the line via Newent to Ledbury on the Hereford–Worcester line. This was opened in July 1885. The lower arm of the signal on the right routes from the Ledbury line to the Docks branch. This signal box was opened in January 1953 with a frame numbered to 58. The unusual design was the result of Gloucestershire CC planning requirements, and it closed in June 1969 under an automation scheme. (*Peter Barlow/Author's Collection*)

Left The final development of GWR signal box equipment inside Over Junction. The lever frame is the standard design and dates from 1926, although it was installed when the box was built in 1953. The levers would have been rusty when they were installed and they are still not 'silver-smooth' yet, five years after installation. The modern block instruments are usually considered to be BR(WR) standard, but were actually designed in 1945-6 at the GWR Signal Works at Reading. Nearest the camera are 'permissive' block instruments for signalling to and from Over Sidings box on the up and down goods loops where more than one train is permitted to occupy the section at any one time. The commutator handle is turned to the left to give 'Line Clear' and can then be turned right through six further positions: 'Train on Line', 2, 3, 4 and 5 trains in section, and 'Blocked Back'. The furthest of the three permissive instruments has 'Train on Line' pegged with the commutator handle in the 'Blocked Back' position. (*Peter Barlow/Author's Collection*)

Above The track diagram. The double track main line at the left-hand end comes from Gloucester West box to Over Sidings box on the right; the Junction signal box is represented by the black rectangle. There is one 'Down Goods Running Loop' and two 'Up Goods Running Loops', about 650 yards long, through to Over Sidings. The Ledbury line is at the bottom of the diagram, the Docks branch at the top. Down trains coming from Gloucester for the Docks branch stopped with the van clear of the junction trailing point. Then the road was set. Interlocking lever 36 reversed, point lever 20, branch crossover 18, discs 22 and 21. The train was then reversed all the way to the Docks Sidings. A train from the Docks to Gloucester reversed out on to the down main line until the engine was clear of crossover 45, then came forward, through 45, to the up main. (*Peter Barlow/Author's Collection*)

Above left Over Junction, levers 44 to 58, the latter being the up distant. On the shelf, the left-hand bell communicates with Over Sidings box and the right-hand with Newent on the single line branch, the electric key token instrument for which can be seen. The double track Docks branch, 638 yards long, was worked by 'telephone and electrical control instruments', to quote the BR(WR) working manual. Permission to move between Over Junction and the Docks Sidings was obtained from the Over Junction signalman or from the Docks Sidings Inspector by telephone according to the direction of the train. Down trains were those going *from* Docks Sidings to Over Junction. The down line starting signal at the Sidings seems to have been locked by 'Interlocking lever 16', marked on the Over Junction diagram as 'Interlocking lever for Down Line, from Docks'. Lever 35 was the interlocking lever for up trains, those going *to* the Docks Sidings. When this was reversed it may have locked signals at the Sidings and released the relevant signal — 36 on the Newent branch, 37 on the up main or 48 on the down main — routing to the Docks branch. At the extremity of the shelf is a bank of four signal arm repeaters for the up main distant signals controlled by lever 58. (*Peter Barlow/Author's Collection*)

Left The Over Junction–Newent electric key token instrument with a key token up in the lock, some token carriers on the hook and the box hand-lamp on the window-sill. The signalman at Newent had to send an electrical release before the man at Over Junction could remove the key token; it was then placed in its cradle on the hooped carrier and the whole contraption could then be either handed up to the train driver or left on a special lineside post to be collected by the fireman as he went past. (*Peter Barlow/Author's Collection*)

Above Over Sidings in 1955, an 1896 box still with its old instruments but with a new frame installed in October 1941, numbered to 41. This box was 659 yards west of Over Junction. The layout was equipped with a facing point outside the box from the down main to both up loops, so that the signalman was allowed to run a freight train into either of these. The down train regained the down main through another facing crossover (see overleaf). Note the circular 'lever collars' hanging from their hooks on the block shelf. The box was closed with Over Junction. (*Peter Barlow/Author's Collection*)

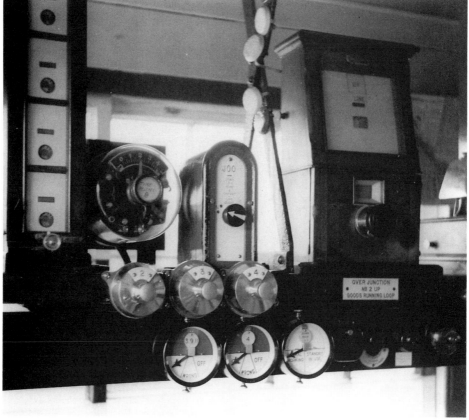

Above left Part of the diagram and instrument shelf at Over Sidings in 1955. The triple array of points from No 2 up loop to the down main shows up well. The inset of double track, in the bottom right-hand corner of the diagram, is to show the down intermediate block signals, the home signal of which was 2 miles 1,544 yards from Over Sidings box. This 'IB' section was half a mile short of the old Oakle Street signal box and carried out its 'break section' function. A Spagnoletti double line block telegraph instrument stands in the centre with a time release in a glass case to the left and the 'Block Switch' (to switch the signal box out of circuit) to the left of that. The purpose of the glass-cased timer was to prevent the signalman from altering the facing points too soon should he put the junction signal back to 'Danger' in front of a train. The signalman could throw the signal lever back far enough to put the arm itself to 'Danger', but the lever was held in a notch in the frame until the electric timer had been started and had taken 2 minutes to run down, whereupon the electric lock holding the signal lever was released. When the lever was restored to the frame the mechanical interlocking was released, permitting the point lever to be operated. The brass plungers numbered 28, 29, 31, 32 and 33 were pressed to operate the electric locks on signals 28 and 29 and point levers 31, 32 and 33. The plungers' electric circuits ran through track circuits, and if these were occupied by a train or vehicle the plungers would not operate the electric locks. (*Peter Barlow/Author's Collection*)

Left At the other end of the shelf, on the left is a GWR four-bank distant signal repeater on the down line. Next to the timer for No 9 signal is the BR(WR) switch to operate the Oakle Street IB signals, No 100. At present the switch shows that the IB home signal is at 'Danger' and its distant signal at 'Caution'. Having obtained 'Line Clear' from Grange Court, the Over Sidings signalman could turn the switch over to clear the colour-light signals. Next to this is a GWR/Tyers 'permissive' block instrument doing the same job as those in Over Junction — but doing it more picturesquely. (*Peter Barlow/Author's Collection*)

Above Ledbury, on the Hereford side of the Malvern Hills between Hereford and Worcester, was the junction for Newent and Over Junction. The box was a tall brick building by contractors McKenzie & Holland for the GWR, and was opened in 1885; its non-GWR origin is shown here by the ceiling. Originally it had a 41-lever McKenzie & Holland frame, but in 1910 it was given a GWR twist frame of 42 levers, the addition being numbered '0'. This frame was later re-locked with a horizontal tappet system below floor level.

There is a Webb-Thompson large electric staff instrument by the door for the section to Dymock, and a small electric key token instrument is also present for working the 'long section' when Dymock was switched out. On the shelf nearest the camera is the famous 'Lock and Block' instrument. At the time of the photograph (1955) there were only four of these, at Ledbury Station, Ledbury Tunnel North End, Colwall and Malvern Wells Tunnel boxes. Owing to reductions in signal boxes only two now exist, at Ledbury Station and Malvern Wells. Opposite the instrument on the stove and the top of the locker are various bits of essential domesticity. (*Peter Barlow/Author's Collection*)

Top Ledbury's 'block shelf' with, on the left, a Spagnoletti instrument to Ashperton, on the Hereford side, and the 'Lock and Block' to Ledbury Tunnel North End box, going towards Malvern and Worcester. Down trains were those coming from Worcester and 'Line Clear' indications for these were shown on the lower dial; the signalman turned the central commutator handle to send 'Line Clear' and thus unlock the down starting signal at Ledbury North End. No further 'Line Clears' could then be sent until the first train had come through the section and operated a treadle on the rail. However, there was an enormous 'Achilles heel' to this — and to all 'Lock and Block' systems. To allow for the occasions when a train was signalled forward and then was unable to proceed, there were release levers placed to the left and right of the main dials, one for 'knocking off' the 'Line Clear', and one for clearing the 'Train on Line'. The whole safety system could thus be over-ridden simply by flicking over the cancelling lever. (*Peter Barlow/Author's Collection*)

Above The last levers in the Ledbury frame, Nos 39, 'Down Main Starting', 40, 'Down Main Home', and 41, 'Down Main Distant'. Beyond that are the detonator-placers — two separate levers in their own frame. Against the wall is the 'hurdy-gurdy' or hand generator for making current to work the motor point and its bolt, lever 35, the facing points in the branch line forking to the up or down main. (*Peter Barlow/Author's Collection*)

All up freight trains were assumed to require assistance from Ledbury to Cummings Crossing box unless they 'whistled up' when passing Stoke Edith to indicate otherwise. Passenger trains also occasionally required assistance from Ledbury. The gradient northwards from Ledbury station and through the 1,323-yard-long single track tunnel to Colwall was slightly over 4 miles at 1 in 70 to 1 in 80, except for a very brief downhill respite past Cummings Crossing box, halfway between Ledbury and Colwall.

The clearance between the roof of the tunnel and the engine's chimney, and between the walls and the sides of the train, was merely a few inches; it was not possible to extend the whole length of a footplate hand-brush between the cabside and the wall. Spare a thought then for the crews of the Ledbury banker who spent several years of their career working back and forth through this 'hell-hole', confined within the sweltering heat of the cab, half choked by the enormous volume of their exhaust fumes thrown down upon them from the close-fitting concave walls of the tunnel.

The banker was supplied from Hereford shed, a '52xx' or '31xx' tank engine which always travelled bunker-first up the hill so that its crew did not have to breath the fumes from two furiously blasting, hard-working engines with the tunnel roof only 12 inches above their volcanic chimneys. Men working tank engines had not even the slight means of escape open to those working tender engines. On these the fireman would create a big fire in the 'box, the driver would set the engine furiously to work, full regulator and 45 per cent cut-off, and both would lie down on the footplate breathing the air from the gap between the engine and the tender. It was as well to bear in mind the disappearing fire and put some more on before it was all thrown out of the chimney.

The atmosphere of the tunnel was particularly dense at the Ledbury end, as if the smoke fell downhill. So dense it was that drivers of down trains could not see daylight at the Ledbury end at a range of 100 yards, and a noisy 'clapper', operated by the vehicle wheels passing over a treadle, was fixed at that distance from the tunnel mouth. Ledbury's down home signal, just visible in this 1955 view, was a 'centre pivot' arm a few feet outside the tunnel mouth and more or less invisible, in damp or rainy weather, with smoke swirling around it.

This '63xx' Class 2-6-0, power class 'D', was permitted to take a maximum of 336 tons — 11 coaches — unassisted through the tunnel in 1936, only two coaches less than a 'Castle'. The same engine hauling freight could take '35 of coal' or 53 wagons of general merchandise. The banker was not coupled to the rear of the train it was assisting unless assistance was required through to Colwall; normally the banker remained uncoupled and dropped off at Cummings Crossing to set back into a 'Middle Siding' and await a path down through the tunnel again. When passenger trains were assisted, the Ledbury engine was coupled to the front.

This is the Ledbury signalman's view as he and the driver of the train wait for the banker to come on the rear. The double line merges to a single track at the mouth of the tunnel, and as soon as the last vehicle of any up train had cleared those points, the signalman at once set the facing points for the down line so that in the event of a breakaway in the tunnel the runaway vehicles would be diverted on to the correct line. (*Peter Barlow/Author's Collection*)

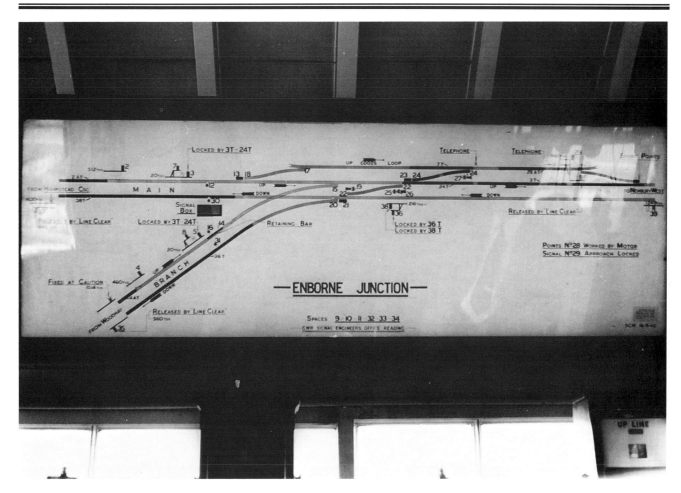

Above left Enborne Junction, 1¼ miles west of Newbury station, looking towards Newbury in 1955. This was where the single track Didcot, Newbury & Southampton (DN&S) line left the westbound main line and turned south for Winchester. The box was opened in about 1907 (replacing an earlier box) and then had a 21-lever frame to work a simple junction. In 1942 the line as far as the next block post, Woodhay, 2¼ miles away, was doubled and an up loop was added alongside the up main line. For this the signal box was given a 39-lever frame. Here we see the signal box's up home signals on main and branch, with Newbury West's distant signals and the signal routing into the up goods loop. (*Peter Barlow/Author's Collection*)

Left The interior of Enborne Junction showing three Spagnoletti instruments. The nearest communicates with Hampstead Crossing, towards Hungerford, the central one is to Woodhay and the farthest one is to Newbury West. The lever with the short handle is No 28, operating the power points at the far end of the loop. Judging by the small churn at the far end of the frame, Enborne Junction's signalmen had their drinking water delivered by train once a day. It is very likely that they also had no toilet facilities beyond an 'Elsan' bucket. Morale, however, is high because the box is spotlessly clean and polished. (*Peter Barlow/Author's Collection*)

Above The track diagram. The facing points from the up main to the loop were track circuited so that they could not be moved once the circuit was occupied by the wheels of a train, and to prevent these points being moved whilst a train was approaching there was a treadle-type 'fouling bar' in the up branch line, just behind the signal box. Whilst this bar was depressed by the flanges of a train's wheels, the facing point bolt lever could not be moved, and thus the 'facers' were locked in whatever position they were at that moment. This device was in lieu of a track circuit, and one wonders if wartime shortages forced the use of such an antique system. (*Peter Barlow/Author's Collection*)

Above left The 1942-style bracket signal at the Newbury end of the up loop at Enborne Junction in 1955. Several of these distinctive structures were erected — at Challow in 1953 and at Hinksey South in 1942, for instance. The ringed arm is the exit signal from the loop, and attached to it are about eight wires operating circuits for 'lamp in/out' repeaters and 'arm on/off' repeaters. The main-line arms are by Westinghouse who also supplied the hand generator and point motors. (*Peter Barlow/Author's Collection*)

Left The Tyers No 1 tablet instrument — modified to permit a tablet which has been removed to be restored to the same instrument — in Sutton Bridge Station box of the Midland & Great Northern Joint Railway in 1956. Hanging on hooks are the hoops and leather pouches for delivering the tablet to the locomotivemen as they pass by on their engine. The instrument controls the single track section to Sutton Bridge East box, but the brass tablets are engraved 'Cross Keys Bridge' — the swing-bridge crossing the River Nene. One tablet was removed — after a co-operative signalling routine between the two signalmen — by pulling out the lowest drawer of the instrument. An incoming tablet, delivered from a passing train, was inserted through a lid in the top of the instrument, again after due co-operation between the two signalmen. To prevent the tablet from falling in anything but a prefectly horizontal position there are three 'check' slides. The lever frame is an ancient Midland Railway production with 'tumbler' locking and levers at 6-inch centres. (*Dr Ian Scrimgeour/Courtesy Signalling Record Society*)

Above The Tyer's tablet instruments at Kinneil signal box, North British Railway, in 1956. On the right is a No 1 showing the top lid through which the incoming tablet was replaced in the machine. This instrument worked the normal block section through to Birkhill. The one on the left is a No 6 machine for working the 'long section' to Bo'ness Junction when Birkhill is switched out. Between the two machines is the draw-slide switch which cuts the 'short section' (No 1 type) instrument out of circuit and brings in the 'long section' (No 6 type) machine. The lever on the left-hand side of the No 6 instrument was lifted to release the bottom slide for an incoming tablet to be replaced in the machine, and again to lift that tablet up into the rest of the stack of tablets. (*Dr Ian Scrimgeour/Courtesy Signalling Record Society*)

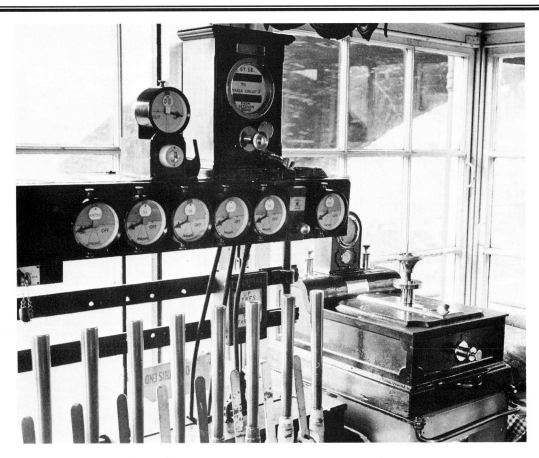

Left A fascinating corner of Reedham Junction box, between Norwich and Yarmouth/Lowestoft, in 1956. The large wooden instrument on the shelf is a Sykes Lock and Block, used to control the approach of up trains from Reedham Swing Bridge to Reedham Junction. The instrument was electrically and mechanically interlocked with the up starting signal lever at Reedham Swing Bridge and Junction; the down-rods from the instrument to the levers can be seen behind the levers. When a train which had been signalled from Reedham Swing Bridge had passed over and depressed a treadle situated a train's length beyond the starting signal at Reedham Junction, the movement of the treadle moved the rods to unlock the instrument and leave it ready to accept the next up train, the lock coming off with an audible 'clank'.

The instrument on the right was a Tyer's No 5 tablet modified to work 'permissively', but this does not have its usual, goods line, meaning — the section was *not* permitted to be occupied by more than one train at a time. Under normal traffic conditions, the 7¼-mile single track block section was from Reedham Junction to Breydon Junction, and the tablets were thus engraved.

On summer Saturdays, race days and Bank Holidays, there was an exceptionally heavy 'tidal flow' of traffic into Yarmouth in the mornings and out of Yarmouth in the evening, and in 1937 traffic was expedited by installing a block post at the remote marshland halt of Berney Arms to halve the 7¼-mile block section. Berney Arms signal box was a shed-like affair with a Tyer's three-position block instrument and two bells to work with Reedham and Breydon, two levers to work a stop signal in each direction and a 'King' lever to switch the block post out of circuit and to disarrange the interlocking so that both stop signals could be lowered. The distant signals were fixed at 'Caution' and had no levers.

With Berney Arms switched in, the Reedham Junction tablet instrument was still released by Breydon Junction, and vice versa, but the starting signals at each place were locked at 'Danger' until released by 'Line Clear' from Berney Arms via the ordinary Tyers block instrument.

The tablet working was 'permissive' in that if a second train arrived at Reedham before the first had cleared Berney Arms, a second tablet could be removed from the instrument before the first tablet had been replaced in the instrument at Breydon, but the starting signal could not be lowered for the second train to leave Reedham until the first train had cleared Berney Arms and another 'Line Clear' had been received from that place.

The tablets were engraved Reedham Junction – Breydon Junction and when Berney Arms was switched out they could be used for up or down trains. But when 'permissive' working was in force, the Reedham or Breydon signalman was responsible for attaching by padlock to each tablet pouch a metal plaque engraved with the legend 'To Breydon Only' or 'To Reedham Only'. This made the tablet valid in one direction only.

The tablet instruments were interlinked so that no tablet could be withdrawn from the instrument at Breydon until all the tablets removed from the Reedham instrument had been placed in the Breydon instrument. The No 5 tablet instruments remained in use until 1972 when they were superceded by electric key token working. (*Dr Ian Scrimgeour/Courtesy Signalling Record Society*)

Left Salisbury 'C' — GWR — box was opened in May 1900 with a 95-lever locking frame (see page 101). Notice how very long are the floor-plates or 'sweeps', due to the large amount of cumbersome GWR 'twist' interlocking machinery under the floor. Instead of GWR brasses many of the levers have Southern Region oval, plastic badges probably dating from 1972 when the frame was reduced to 65 levers and re-locked due to the abolition of the Western Region goods yard. The box closed in 1973.

Right The GWR lines approaching Salisbury in 1972 with the GWR 1942-vintage steel bracket signal cleared for the route into the Southern station. 'C' box is in the middle distance.

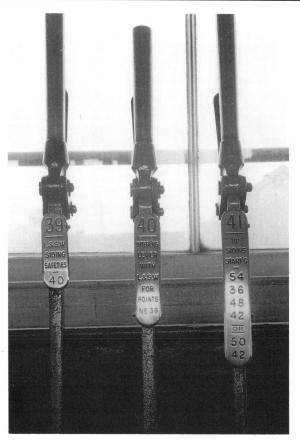

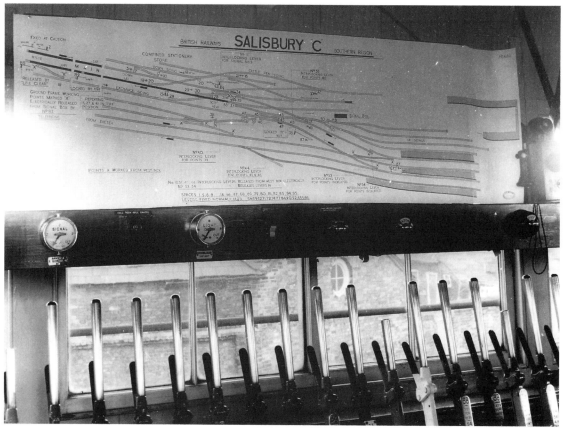

Above left GWR lever brasses in Salisbury 'C' which date from 1900. No 39 lever operated 'L&SW Siding Safeties', trap points preventing movements from the Southern Region up sidings on to or across the WR/SR junction into the Western Region sidings. No 40 is the 'Interlocking lever with L&SW for Points No 39'. Before the traps could be closed to permit this movement, lever 40 had to be reversed and that could not be done until the SR signalman in West box had given an electrical release.

Left The diagram in 1972 showing the 'LSWR' station in the bottom right-hand corner with the junctions across to the 'GWR' side. There is an ominous empty space above the former; this is the site of the GWR station now bereft of any rails. Even after the passenger service from Westbury ceased, the GWR station was used for goods work until the yard was abolished in 1972 — hence the reduction of the frame by 30 levers. As we have seen there were several 'interlocking levers' to control each end of the WR/SR junction. For example, before the SR's West box man could reverse the point from the down SR to the WR, the WR signalman had to reverse interlocking lever 53, and before the WR signalman could reverse the opposite end of the same junction track — point 45 — he had to reverse lever 44 which was locked electrically from West box. There were a good many special bell codes between the SR West box and the WR 'C' box to enable these complicated routines to be effected, but the SR and WR men co-operated very well. They used to watch the doors on each other's passenger trains so that both sides of the train were checked and they also used to watch each other's tail-lamps. The 'C' box signalman used to be able to give 'Train out of Section' to the next WR box along the line before he had seen the tail-lamp because the West box man would see it and 'give him the tip'.

Above The signalling at Salisbury (LSWR) was done by the Westinghouse electro-pneumatic system, brought into use here in November 1902. The friendly signalman in Salisbury West box in 1972 took the covers off to show me the tappet interlocking between his Westinghouse draw-slides. The slide was a 'cam-plate', with handle attached. If the interlocking permitted, the slide could be pulled out and at the end of its travel electrical contacts were 'made' which opened the air valve to that point or signal cylinder. Interlocking between slides, as between conventional levers, was essential to prevent a conflicting movement being signalled, so when the slide was pulled out, the inclined slot cut through it (the 'cam-plate' action) drove downwards the vertical tappet blade to which it was connected. The movement of the blade displaced the locks — the small blocks of metal seen here — which were forced sideways into recesses cut into other tappet blades which were thereby locked. The sideways motion of the lock was by means of a 'bridle iron' which communicated with any other locks which required to be moved to lock or unlock other tappet blades and their slides. This brief — and necessarily sketchy — description applies to tappet locking generally and, I hope, gives the general idea of what it is about.

Above far left Salisbury West box up home signals and East box's distant signals in 1972. The latticework mast and 'dolls' are ex-LSWR, the arms BR(SR) upper quadrants. In the left distance can be seen the ex-GWR junction signal reading 'To SR' (right-hand arms) and 'To GW station' (left hand) (see page 165).

Above left The view eastwards from the London end of the down platform towards Salisbury East box in 1972. The air cylinder which operates the arm can be seen on the right of the mast below the 'track circuit' diamond sign. The sign indicates to the engine crew that the presence of their train/engine is indicated in the signal box through the track circuit system.

Left The vintage air pressure gauges in Salisbury East box. The left-hand dial gives the pressure in the pipelines to the various signal and point cylinders — 15 lbs per sq in — while the other gives the pressure in the main pipe from the pump house — 28 lbs per sq in. There are a pair of very beautiful bells, one working with the East Yard shunters, the other with Tunnel Junction signal box, and some highly polished bell plungers — doubtless all dating from 1902. On the diagram can be seen Salisbury East's up starting signals which are also Tunnel Junction's home signals, directing to Waterloo and Southampton.

Above The power frame in Salisbury East had draw-slides numbered to 63 set in a cabinet of very highly polished wood. The whole place was exceptionally well kept. The West box had an authentic air of well-rubbed-in, well-polished sootiness, a certain gloominess of interiors associated with the passing of countless 'T9' and 'King Arthur' Class engines, but in East box the honey-coloured teak console was electric-clean and polished, the room light and airy, a very different atmosphere which was quite surprising in a building which had stood beside an intensively used steam railway for 63 years.

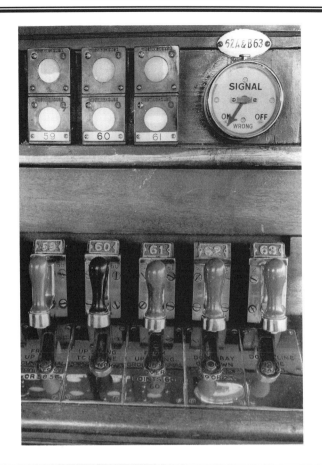

Above left A close-up of the last few slides in the frame, their undersides reflected in the glass-smooth brasses beneath. This phenomenon recalls the famous brass plate which was set into the pavement outside the Guard Room of the regimental depot of the Black Watch — younger railway enthusiasts ask your grandfather to explain. Note the gleaming grain of the tropical teak console.

Left Salisbury Tunnel Junction box was erected to the LSWR's design during the 1870s when block signalling was first installed here. The style is reminiscent of an ordinary dwelling house, complete with lean-to storehouse/toilet. The earliest known GWR signal box design follows a very similar pattern. This 1972 view shows what was probably its original nameboard, and the box gave continuous service until it was destroyed in a signalling modernisation scheme in August 1981.

Above The interior of Tunnel Junction in 1972. Preece's two-position instrument operated from Dean, on the Romsey line. The upright wooden handle enabled the Tunnel Junction signalman to operate the semaphore arm in the corresponding instrument at Dean, The brass plunger labelled 'Dean' operated the bell in Dean signal box. When Dean rang 'Is Line Clear?' to Tunnel Junction, the latter signalman pulled the handle forward, casing the semaphore arm in the Dean instrument to drop. When Dean sent 'Train entering Section' to Tunnel Junction, the latter restored the handle, which caused the arm in Dean's instrument to return to 'Danger'. The other four instruments are Sykes 'Lock and Block'. The instrument at the far end unlocked the Up Line starting signal at Salisbury East; the central pair locked the Dean line home and starting; the fourth was worked from Salisbury East to unlock Tunnel Junction's Down Line starting signal. In 1968 the main line to Andover was fully track circuited and equipped with automatic colour-lights. Tunnel Junction's Up Main starting signal was then unlocked automatically when the track circuits were clear a sufficient distance ahead.

Above left The lever frame in Tunnel Junction, with lever 'A' furthest from the camera. The original frame was numbered 1-20, and lever 'A' was added in April 1910 to release electrically a lever in a ground frame working a set of points leading from Salisbury East Yard to the up main immediately outside the west end of Fisherton tunnel. Levers 4 and 5, spare here (painted white), probably once worked the up main and up branch inner homes situated just inside Fisherton tunnel at the east end. Lever 'A' was taken out of use in July 1950 when the above-mentioned East Yard ground frame was connected to the electro-pneumatic system operated from East box.

Left A Western Region gantry, erected some time after 1956, carrying Aller Junction's home signals on the down relief line (right-hand track) and the down main, second from right. This replaced a pair of wooden GWR three-'doll' brackets. The arms form two groups of three, reading, from the left as we look at them: No 45 Down main; No 43 Down Main to Down Goods Loop; No 40, Down Main to Branch; No 44 Down Relief to Down Main; No 35 Down Relief to Down Goods Loop; No 38 Down Relief to Branch. The view is towards Newton Abbot in 1971.

Above Looking west from the same bridge reveals the tracks and junctions referred to, and Aller Junction signal box.

Right Dainton Tunnel signal box stood a few yards west of the 264-yard-long tunnel and slightly below the summit of the most famous incline on the GWR. The tracks rose at gradients varying between 1 in 71 and 1 in 36 for the 2½ miles from Aller Junction and were almost as steep for the 2 miles westwards to Totnes. The signal box housed a 17-lever frame and was most important as a 'break section' box and the place where the banking engines, having assisted a freight train up the grade, were crossed over to the other line to run back to the foot of the bank.

There was little traffic regulating done here, other than controlling the bank engines, because the up refuge siding held 27 wagons and the down refuge 32, both too short to hold many of the freight trains. The down refuge was unusual in that instead of reversing into it, trains ran in directly, through facing points 8, and reversed out. These sidings were mostly used for stabling the banking engine until a suitable 'path' presented itself for the run back down the incline to its Aller Junction or Totnes base.

Providing that the weather was clear, the Aller Junction bank engine was not coupled to the rear of the down freight train it was assisting, but 'dropped off' the train near the eastern tunnel portal and stopped until the signalman rang the very loud bell fixed by the lineside just there. This indicated to the enginemen that the line through the tunnel was clear and that the driver could proceed to the down home signal.

When assisting freight trains from Totnes, the bank engine was always coupled to the brake van, for these up freights always stopped at the stop board just beyond the eastern tunnel portal to pin down brakes and to allow the bank engine to be uncoupled. The banker then ran back through the tunnel without further signals and came to a stand at the ground disc signal just inside the west end. Having come to a stand, the engine whistled '3 short–1 crow' to indicate it was at a stand, whereupon the signalman moved the points for whatever route he had selected.

The signal box is a Saxby & Farmer construction dating from about 1874 and houses a frame of levers numbered 1-17. It was superceded in February 1965 by a Western Region 'plywood wonder' signal box with 21 levers, and this was in turn abolished by the automated signalling scheme based at Exeter in May 1985. In this 1955 photograph, a Southern 'Spam can', No 34061 *73 Squadron*, shuffles up the 1 in 37 with seven ex-GWR coaches. The gradient of the main line can be seen by the dead level of the sidings on each side. What a fantastic place to work — in any weather, warm summer sunshine as here or drenching rain, remote in the hills with a constant procession of steam engines struggling with the gradient! Never mind the lack of a toilet and running water! (*Peter Barlow/Author's Collection*)

Left The layout at Aller Junction in 1956 with the up and down main lines to Plymouth going to the top left, the double track branch to Torquay and Kingswear going straight on to the left and the quadruple track to Newton Abbot to the right. The up main line is the topmost track, the up relief is next below, then the down main and, at the bottom, the down relief line. There are two trains present, indicated by electric lights on the track diagram — one on the up main line and one in the down goods loop off the down main. There is a bank engine spur at the end of the loop permitting the assisting engine to go on to the rear of a goods train requiring assistance. This layout, signal box and frame numbered 1-46 were installed in May 1925 as part of the Newton Abbot station enlargement scheme.

In May 1929 there was a rear-end collision on the up main at the spot indicated by the twin lamps. A goods train had come down Dainton bank and had stopped on the up main ahead of signal 3/8 while the guard took off the wagon hand-brakes. The Aller Junction signalman had seen the tail-lamp so he gave 'Line Clear' to Dainton (or Stoneycombe if it was switched in) for the 7.10 am Plymouth–Newton Abbot passenger train, which he was entitled to do. He also gave 'Line Clear' to Kingskerswell for a passenger train off the branch and 'got the road' for this train from Newton Abbot West, on the up relief line. When he went to lower the up relief line signals for the Kinskerswell train, there being no 'sequential locking' and no track circuits, he pulled the up relief starting signal and then inadvertently pulled the up main inner home, home and distant signals, with the result that No 4909 *Blakesley Hall*, a Plymouth Laira engine and brand new, crashed into the freight's brake van, killing the guard. The track circuit seen illuminated on the up main in this picture was then installed to lock at 'Danger' the up main inner home signal to the rear. (*Peter Barlow/Author's Collection*)

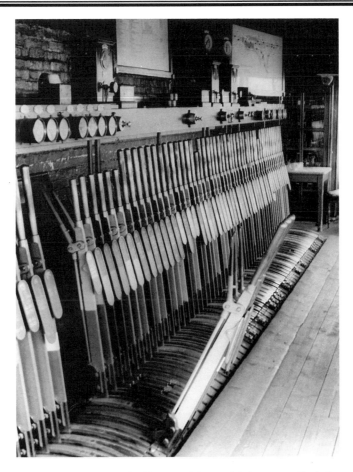

Above left A signal box with a fine view — Royal Albert Bridge, which controlled the merging of the double track main line to single track over the magnificent Brunelian bridge and the exit from the down passenger avoiding line from St Budeaux West. This building was erected in 1908 to house a frame of 15 levers, only eight working. In June 1952 it was given a new 25-lever frame with a hand generator to operate two sets of motor points to take over the operation of the facing points to the down passenger avoiding line and a trailing crossover formerly controlled by St Budeaux West.

During the Second World War the river Tamar here was full of moored warships protected by barrage balloons. The latter sometimes broke from their moorings and drifted silently through the air, dragging their wire hawsers across land and water and causing great damage — especially to the railway telegraph wires. On 24 August 1942 an incident occurred where a drifting barrage balloon dragged its long wire 'tail' across the steel walls of the approach spans of the Royal Albert Bridge. The hawser wedged in the vertical gap between two plate girders and drew taut across the track at buffer-beam height. Luckily Signalman Trethewey was walking across the bridge from Saltash to the Royal Albert Bridge signal box, saw the cable, realised that a passenger train was due and ran as fast as he could to the box to warn his mate — who had already given 'Line Clear'. If the engine had hit that steel cable it would at the very least have been derailed, or at worst it could have brought down the approach spans, with a very long drop on to houses below. The signal box was abolished under automation in July 1973. Photographed in 1955. (*Peter Barlow/Author's Collection*)

Left Minster station was opened in April 1846 on the line from Ashford to Margate and became a junction in 1847 when the branch southwards to Sandwich and Deal was opened. Block signalling arrived many years later and this box was opened in 1926, when a connecting chord was laid from the Margate to the Sandwich line to the west of the signal box, thus forming a triangular junction all controlled from here. Although built new under Southern Railway auspices, the building, photographed in 1957, seems to be of SE&CR design. Only the name of the railway had changed in 1921 — the same men were in the drawing office. (*Peter Barlow/Author's Collection*)

Above The interior of Minster signal box held a Westinghouse 'A2' pattern 70-lever frame and is spartan, without linoleum on the floor and with surprisingly dirty lever handles. There is no lever-pulling duster to be seen and the grimy lever handles suggest none was used. (*Peter Barlow/Author's Collection*)

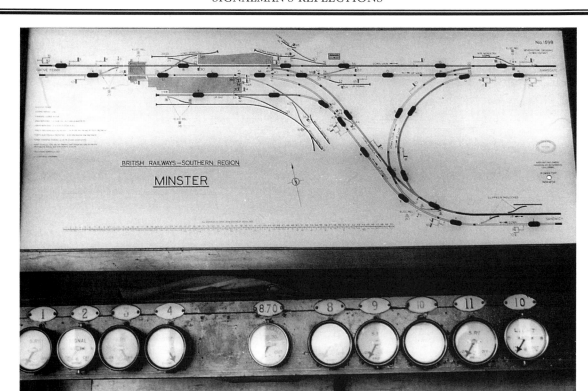

Above left The Minster signalman had a really worthwhile and interesting job, controlling a complex and busy layout with his traditional equipment. The diagram shows the track coming in from Ashford/Canterbury West and the Charing Cross–Dover main line (left-hand side) and going out to Ramsgate and Broadstairs, whereafter it curved back on itself, through Margate and along the North Kent coast to rejoin the Charing Cross line at Faversham. The fork to the bottom right at the base of the triangle is the tracks to Sandwich, Deal and Dover. (*Peter Barlow/Author's Collection*)

Left Banbury Hump Yard ground frame was a prince amongst ground frames — one normally thinks of them as little wooden huts, holding three levers. It was opened in July 1931 and held a 10-lever McKenzie & Holland frame to work points and signals in the Reception Sidings and a Descubes Patent electro-pneumatic push-button console of 21 buttons working the points in the sorting sidings at the foot of the hump. An early diesel shunter is seen in this 1955 view at the top of the slope over which it steadily pushed long rafts of trucks which the shunters uncoupled so that they free-wheeled down into the chosen siding until all was carefully sorted into fresh trains. The electro-pneumatic system of point operation was perfect for this situation because the point blades snapped over instantaneously in front of the rolling wagons when the button was pressed. The operator and shunter worked in concert to switch each raft into the correct siding. (*Peter Barlow/Author's Collection*)

Above The reception sidings, points and signals controlled from Banbury Hump ground frame, looking north to Banbury Junction with the Paddington–Birmingham main line on the far left. All three signals are motor worked; the lowered arm routes from the reception sidings to the engine line and to the station, the other two route to the hump. (*Peter Barlow/Author's Collection*)

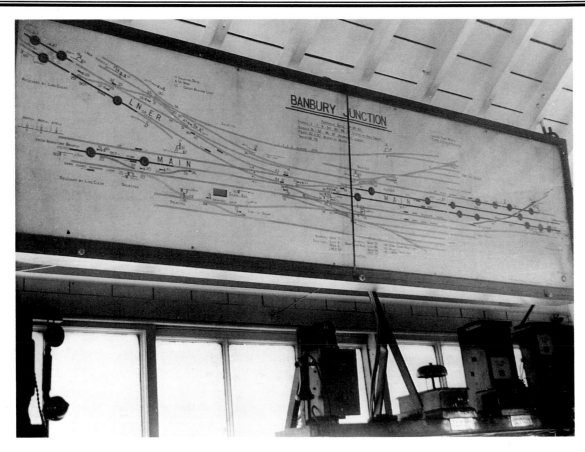

Above left The layout controlled by the signalman at Banbury Junction, with the GCR/LNER running in from Woodford Halse at the top left. The box was opened in 1900 and housed a lever frame numbered 1-75, extended to 98 in 1940. The relative lack of track circuits is worth noting; only the heavy black lines indicate track circuited lengths and the large black circles on these lines are windows through which white lights shine when that length is occupied. This huge and apparently vital installation was completely abolished in March 1980.

Left The Isle of Man is, literally, a 'law unto itself', and its railways were marvellously idiosyncratic. This 1955 view is entering Douglas station from a train on the single track coming in from Port Erin with the right-hand arm lowered — lever 16 in the 'Points Cabin' — to take it into the Port Erin line platform. The signal below this, lever 17, routed trains to the goods yard. The adjacent single track is to and from Peel, whence a train is also expected. The Ruritanian signal is by Duttons and dates from the 1870s. In the distance the 'Points Cabin' can be seen together with the outgoing signals for the Port Erin/Peel lines mounted on a bracket. (*Peter Barlow/Author's Collection*)

Above What appears to be the signal box at Douglas was always referred to by the staff and by official books as the 'Points Cabin'. The design and installation of the signalling on the Island was officially the work of signalling contractors Dutton & Co, whose representative for the Isle of Man contract was Mr O'Donnell. The latter had his own ideas about design and did his best to have them adopted rather than those of Mr Dutton. Consequently there was a very great deal of argument between the two men with the Isle of Man railways in the middle. As the railway company's minute put it: 'It would appear that Messrs Dutton and O'Donnell do not agree'. The Douglas cabin came out as a hybrid design, part Dutton, part O'Donnell, as each man tried to superimpose his ideas on the other. (*Peter Barlow/Author's Collection*)

Above left The exceedingly spartan interior of Douglas 'Points Cabin' in 1955 with a frame of Dutton's patent levers. The locking was driven by the lever handle — note the drive-rod going down the front of the lever. The signalman pulls the handle which comes to the upright position, in line with the rest of the lever, and instantly displaces the interlocking via the down-rod. He then pulls the lever across until it is fully reversed and stops against the frame casting, whereupon the lever handle pivots forward and completes the movement of the interlocking below the floor. Apart from a pair of distant signal arm repeaters there are no instruments here. The signalling instruments — GPO 'single-needle' telegraph instruments — are in the Station Master's office. (*Peter Barlow/Author's Collection*)

Left Grayrigg signal box was 46 miles north of Preston and approximately 7 miles north-west of Oxenholme at the summit of a 7-mile climb at 1 in 131/106. This box, LNWR in appearance, was opened in 1925-6 when the LMS installed up and down goods loops here. I spent some weeks here on a 'busman's holiday' taking time off from my own signal box to work this one. It was surrounded by magnificent countryside with the How Gill moors above the River Lune sometimes blue, sometimes purple, in the western distance. Water for our tea came from a spring in a field on the opposite side of the line. The year is 1966.

Above Steam engines had gone from the Western Region but here they were still working hard in considerable numbers — '8F's, 'Black Fives', '9F' Class 2-10-0s and 'Britannia' 'Pacifics'. Many heavy freight trains were given banking assistance from Oxenholme and after a few days I was able to ride the footplates of the bankers. One Sunday I spent all day on a steam-hauled engineering train on Grayrigg bank, high above the valley, looking from the cab down to a stone-walled farmhouse as we talked railways and drank tea, in between the occasional movement of the engine to re-position the engineering machinery. Railways were very human, they were best for people who enjoyed the ordinary things of life — not ambitious 'whizz-kids' using their mates as a ladder, but steady practical people who put the job first and enjoyed each other's company.

This 1966 view at Grayrigg looks east down the bank with the LNWR up loop starter and Mosedale Hall's distant below and a 'Black Five' raising the echoes as she forges with musical exhaust beat steadily up and over the gradient.

Views from the box. *Above left* Irish railway signalling equipment installed before 1921 and probably for some years after that was made in Britain, and Ireland is now the last refuge of such sensible objects as the Saxby & Farmer-built signal box at Killarney. It houses a 35-lever frame, apparently of Railway Signal Co manufacture. This 1973 view from the box is towards the overall-roofed terminal station, which, whilst having nothing whatever to do with I.K. Brunel, does convey a Brunelian flavour. On the right is the yard, and the line to Tralee, the county town of Kerry. The railway was opened to the Killarney terminus in 1853 and was extended to Tralee six years later. However, the continuation to Tralee diverges from the Killarney line on the east side of the signal box so trains to Tralee must reverse out of Killarney station until the engine is clear of the facing points. Trains from Tralee reverse into Killarney station. This is done with speed and precision born of long habit. The signals in this view are tubular steel CIE productions.

Left The signalman at Kingsbridge had this for his daily view in 1955, a scene barely altered since the gas lamp, bottom left, was erected decades earlier. Like the scene, the men on the job also seemed unchanging. There was a wonderful sense of security in the steady continuity — the peace and quiet — the 'rightness' of it all. We thought it was going to last for ever!

Above The '45' Class tank engine in the previous picture is seen here running round its train. The Kingsbridge signalman has placed a key token in the lock of the instrument working the section to Gara Bridge box, ready for the time when he must 'ask the road', 3-1 on the bell plunger seen alongside the token. When the Gara Bridge signalman replies he will hold his plunger in on the final beat to send a current to release the lock on the key token here. The Kingsbridge signalman will then turn the key anti-clockwise through the lock and pull it out of the instrument, place it in the hooped carrier and give it to the driver as his guarantee of a clear road on the single track. (*Peter Barlow/Author's Collection*)

Above left The lucky signalman's view looking towards Westbury from Castle Cary box as No 4978 *Westwood Hall* comes through at the regulation 60 mph on a London–Plymouth express. 'Cary was at the foot of the 1 in 80 Bruton bank and was situated between two sharp curves, hence the speed restriction. The three-'doll' GWR tubular steel bracket signal routes trains to the West of England (the arm lowered here), to Weymouth or to the loop. Castle Cary box at the time of this 1955 photograph was a 1942 'ARP'-type, all brick with a flat roof to replace the GWR hip-roofed building which was destroyed by a direct hit from a German 'tip and run' raider on 3 September 1942. The bomb killed the signalman, Mr Silbey, and the driver of a shunting engine, Mr Shergold, and also destroyed his engine, 0-6-0 tank No 1729. (*Peter Barlow/Author's Collection*)

Left This was the signalman's view at Ruscombe Sidings box, 1¼ miles east of Twyford, looking towards Paddington in 1955, the express being on the down main line. The adjacent track is the up main, next is a siding, next again is the down relief line with a trailing crossover to the up relief and, on the left-hand edge of the picture, a set of points trailing into the up relief from a siding. The signal to the left of the engine's smokebox is the down relief line home, placed on the 'wrong' side of the track. Ruscombe Sidings box was opened in 1893 with a frame of levers numbered 1-29, extended to 38 in 1913. The box was abolished in October 1961. (*Peter Barlow/Author's Collection*)

Above Brunel laid 8 miles of dead straight track from slightly west of Maidenhead to the west end of Sonning Cutting. The gradient was, as near as makes no difference, level. Galloping 'Down Relief' on the long, level, straight in a scene from my boyhood is a '61-er' making 60 mph with some maroon non-corridor suburban service coaches on an 'A' headcode train. The view is towards London from the little eight-lever 'break section' Shottesbrooke box opened in 1899, 1½ miles east of Ruscombe Sidings. The down main and relief line signals are 'off' — note that the GWR wooden signal on the latter line is on the 'wrong' side of its line so that the two signals are kept as far apart as possible to avoid confusing the drivers of approaching trains. Although such 'break section' signal boxes were tiny, their signalmen were kept very busy 'pulling off and putting back' for at least 90 trains during an early turn, weekday shift, at the time of this photograph, 1955. The density of traffic can be gauged by the fact that the signal boxes between Reading and Slough were spaced at roughly 1½-mile intervals, excluding those at stations where there were two or three in the space of a mile. The remarkable thing is that the technology had existed to replace these little wooden boxes with motor-operated semaphores worked from a larger box since 1905 — and colour-lights could have been used from the late 1920s — but in fact 'break section' signal boxes were still being built in 1934. Shottesbrooke box was abolished in July 1961. (*Peter Barlow/Author's Collection*)

Above far left The 'pole routes' carrying the telegraph and telephone wires were a vital part of the signalling scene. I always found the masts, cross-bars and wires interesting and enjoyed the sound that the wind, even a gentle breeze, made through the wires. There was a great deal of skill required for the lineman to maintain his pole route properly — and at no small risk to himself. This 1970 view is from the rear window of Oxford North Junction, looking north along the old LNWR line to Bicester and Bletchley, the ex-GWR on the extreme left, and the 1942 junction between the two routes in the middle distance.

Above left The insulators in the previous picture were very old indeed, far older than the signal box which was a 1940 GWR 'ARP' production, but on this — to me at any rate — magnificent array at the back of my signal box at Hinksey North, the ceramics are relatively new, probably dating from 1942 when the box and the marshalling yard it controlled were built. Here all the circuits are brought down to the ground then below ground to cross the river Thames without constituting a danger to the swans — a very proper consideration. Very often the wires went over the water and were then threaded through blocks of some material so as to make the otherwise invisible and deadly obstacle formed by the wires obvious to all flying creatures. Photographed in 1969.

Left The Trecwn branch train arrives back 'engine and van' at Letterston Junction in 1955 and stands under the telegraph wires while the men brew up in the signal box before returning home to Fishguard. (*Peter Barlow/Author's Collection*)

Above Just to prove that the signal box could be just as pleasant a place in vile weather, this is the 8.45 am Plymouth to Paddington, hauled by D1012 *Western Firebrand*, seen through the window of Witham box in 1975 as torrential midsummer rain is hurled against the glass by a storm-force wind which was shrieking and howling through the telegraph wires strung between their poles. At such times there was no better place to be than in a signal box — except perhaps out at sea. It was exhilarating and well worth coming to work for.

INDEX